A–Z

OF

COVENTRY

PLACES - PEOPLE - HISTORY

David McGrory

AMBERLEY

Acknowledgements

My thanks go to Rob Orland and John Ashby and for pictures, Barry Denton, Margaret Porter, Roy Baron, Coventry Watch Museum and Coventry City Council. All remaining pictures are from the David McGrory Collection and Rob and Steve Orland.

First published 2018

Amberley Publishing
The Hill, Stroud, Gloucestershire, GL5 4EP
www.amberley-books.com

The right of David McGrory to be identified as the Author of this work has been asserted in accordance with the Copyrights, Designs and Patents Act 1988.

ISBN 978 1 4456 7488 9 (print)
ISBN 978 1 4456 7489 6 (ebook)

British Library Cataloguing in Publication Data. A catalogue record for this book is available from the British Library.

Origination by Amberley Publishing.
Printed in Great Britain.

Contents

Introduction

Not everyone sees it but Coventry is a remarkable city, with remarkable people and a remarkable history. Its history goes back into ancient times; it was the fourth largest city in medieval England and became the home to a royal family, effectively a capital. Its industrial history made it a capital of watchmaking, cycles and motor cars. It suffered one of the most intensive air raids in history and many more raids, yet like a phoenix it rises.

Recently the city won the City of Culture bid for 2021. This was fought mainly on diversity and youth, but culture and history lies deep within Coventry and its remarkable past needs to be brought forward, back into the light. This is an opportunity to put Coventry back on the map and give the people the recognition they deserve.

A close-up of a stained-glass Coventry elephant of great skill with twisted trunk, from the north window of St Mary's Hall.

A

Arms

The arms of Coventry, given in the reign of Edward III, bears imagery that confuses many. I have been told numerous times that the helmet and catamountain (English wild cat) comes off the crest on the Black Prince's helmet; this is not true. Coventry's early coat of arms consisted solely of its motto '*Camera Principis*' ('Prince's Chamber'), the elephant and castle (double symbol of strength) in a shield representing the split diocese of Coventry (red) and Lichfield (green), and the wildcat (watchfulness) standing on top of the shield. The closed helm was added when the city was made a county borough in 1888. The Black Prince did have a cat on his war helm: it was actually a lion. He owned Cheylesmore Manor and his stay there in 1358 is the only reference I can find of him being here. The city motto, of course, doesn't actually refer to Edward as it wasn't in use at that time. It is used in the sense that kings/queens were referred to as princes. It was used to welcome Henry VI to the city a century later: 'Welcome to this your chamber of Princes.' The later supporters the phoenix, representing Coventry rising from the ashes, and the eagle, for Leofric, were added in 1959.

Coventry's civic coat of arms as it is today.

Bablake School

It is claimed that Thomas Wheatley, former mayor, ironmonger and card maker, founded the school in 1563. He sent a servant to Spain to buy steel gads and the barrels arrived full of silver ingots. The servant didn't know the original source and Wheatley kept them, in case of enquiry ... nothing happened. Later he gave the profit from the silver and part of his fortune to charitable purposes, including this school. This was accepted as the source of the school's foundation; it is, however, wrong.

The original school register records the hospital of Bablake was erected in 1560. Bablake School, then called Bablake Hospital, was established in 1560 as a blue coat

Bablake School, on the right, in the Bablake quadrangle.

school by the mayor and council using charitable contributions. Blue coat schools started in the sixteenth century for poor or foundling children. Blue being the colour of charity, the children wore blue coats.

The council administered the school and gave it £40 annually. Recently some have claimed it dates from the fourteenth century. There was an earlier school in the quadrangle attached to the College of St John; this school was set up by the merchants of St Mary's Hall, for guildsmen's children. It was run by the priests and was funded by the guild. That school was dissolved by the Chantries Act of December 1547.

In 1890, Bablake moved to Coundon Road and the boys' uniform – the blue coat, yellow petticoat, stockings and black tasselled cap – was changed for a blue Eaton-style uniform with straw hat. The original building is part of the east range of the Bablake quadrangle and dates from the fifteenth and early sixteenth centuries.

Bicycles

The bicycle trade grew out of the Coventry Sewing Machine Co., founded in 1863 by James Starley and Josiah Turner. In 1868, a French Michaux cycle arrived in Coventry and was tested by Starley's assistant, Edward Cooper. The company, renamed the Coventry Machinists Company, began producing their own version called the 'Coventry Model' and began selling them at home and abroad.

In 1870, Starley set up with William Hillman and began producing improved cycles of their own designs, the first important bicycle being the Ariel, the first lightweight all metal framed, geared small penny-farthing. It became so common it was called the 'Ordinary'. Starley also produced the 'Wonder', for which he invented the differential gear. In 1881, he was commanded to attend the queen with two of his Salvo Quad tricycles. The queen loved them and they were renamed the 'Royal Salvo'. Starley died later that year at his home in Upper Well Street.

In 1876, Harry J. Lawson (later involved in the motor car) created the first chain-driven safety bicycle, followed seven years later by the improved version of the Coventry Lever Tricycle. Starley's nephew John Kemp Starley introduced the modern safety cycle in 1885 called the 'Rover', which had a triangulated frame, pneumatic tyres and wheels of the same diameter and chain drive. The following year Humber opened a factory in Coventry. Coventry's Hillman, Herbert and Cooper's Premier Cycle Company had an annual output in 1897 of 40,000 machines and was the largest cycle manufacturers in the world. They were eclipsed by Rudge-Whitworth who in 1906 produced 75,000 cycles.

By the 1890s over 40,000 people worked in Coventry's cycle trade and between the 1860s and 1930s there were 248 cycle factories in the city. After 1896 a depression set in and the number of Coventry firms dwindled to a few well-established ones such as Bayliss & Thomas, Coventry Eagle, Rudge-Whitworth, Swift and Triumph. Many cycle manufacturers began to produce motor cars and from 1925 competition from

Old James Starley cycles being ridden in the 1952 Godiva procession.

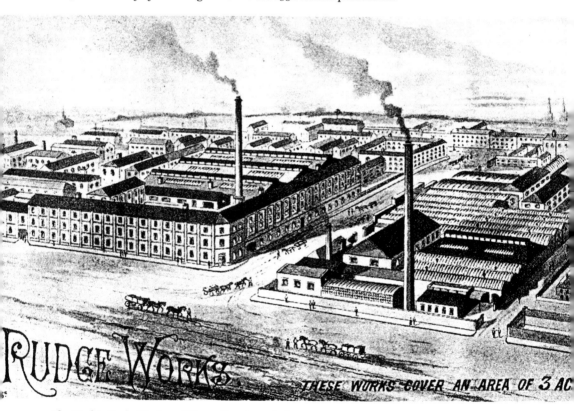

The Rudge Cycle Works, off Spon Street, *c.* 1896.

the motor industry and new production methods led to further decline, and Singer, Swift, Riley and Triumph stopped cycle production. Two companies survived the war: Associated Cycle Manufacturers and Coventry Eagle. The first was taken over by Raleigh in 1954 and the second moved to Smethwick in 1959.

Blitz

The first bombs in the area were on 25 June 1940 when five fell around Ansty Aerodrome. On 18 August the first bombs fell in the city boundary, destroying houses in Canley. Eight days later a short raid left the city's new cinema, the Rex, in ruins, ironically before it was to play *Gone with the Wind*. Three days later the first fatalities came, with sixteen dead in Hillfields. During October there were many small intense raids, leaving 176 dead; among these were the warden, nurse and six inmates of Ford's Hospital. The raids continued.

On 8 November the RAF bombed Munich, the birthplace of the Nazi Party. Hitler sought revenge and Göring suggested Coventry, being compact, would make a good target. Operation Moonlight Sonata was instigated and over 400–500 bombers were brought together. As the night of 14 November closed in, bombers of Kampfgeschwader 100 left France. These were the 'pathfinder' squadron who carried crude computers; they followed radio beams, known as the X-Gerat system, to their target. Each aircraft followed a continuous beam, which broke down if they strayed. As they got nearer a second beam cut through the first, initiating the bombing sequence, then as they approached the centre of Coventry a third beam told the computer to begin its final dropping run.

At 7 p.m. the air-raid sirens began to wail and at 7.20 p.m. the ack-ack and Bofurs burst into life as planes droned overhead in the moonlit sky. First came parachute flares, hanging like white chandeliers. Then incendiaries, normal ones, followed for the first time by exploding phosphorus incendiaries. They fired the target so the other bombers under General Field Marshalls Kesselring and Sperrle could see it.

At 7.30 p.m. the second wave arrived and the first high explosives began to shake the city. Incendiaries fell amid bombs as streams of bombers criss-crossed the city every fifteen minutes. Some hit industrial targets but the majority, as ordered, concentrated on indiscriminately bombing the centre of the city ... to create a firestorm.

The old cathedral was hit by incendiaries and despite valiant efforts its defenders had to leave it to its fate. By 7.59 p.m. all fire appliances in the city were in use. People sheltered in cellars, crypts and air-raid shelters as the city was ripped apart above them. Others stayed at home in Andersons and under the stairs. The bombing continued, with added oil and landmines.

Landmines suspended under parachutes fell silently and exploded above ground sending the blast down and out, flattening anything beneath it. The Church of St Nicholas in Radford was destroyed by one, leaving dead and injured in the crypt

Looking across Broadgate on 15 November 1940.

Coventrians wander down what may have been Much Park Street.

and only one course of stones standing. My father spent the night rescuing the survivors amid the bombs.

At 2 a.m. they still came; by this time with less resistance as most of the air-defence stations had run out of ammunition or the men were simply incapable through exhaustion of loading the shells. Some factories were blasted and burning, suburban streets were littered with rubble as houses were blasted into them. The city centre was one great blaze: flames leapt 100 feet into the sky; bombers 150 miles away could see the glow ahead. The last dozen bombs fell in Shortly Road at 5.30 a.m. At 6.15 a.m. the all-clear sounded and slowly the stunned people emerged into what had once been their streets.

The city was shrouded in smoke, it was drizzling and people wandered amid the destruction. There were 2,294 homes destroyed, 5,602 uninhabitable, 29,374 damaged and thirty-five factories damaged. Among the rubble lay human remains – some were never identified. A total of 568 men, women and children lay dead and 863 were severely injured. It was a miracle the figure wasn't higher considering the city had been hit by 30,000 incendiaries, 500 tons of high explosive, fifty landmines and twenty oil mines for eleven long hours. Cats had left the city, the dogs stayed and amazingly birds sang amid the smoking ruins. The world had never witnessed this sort of airborne devastation; the Germans coined a new word for it 'coventrated'.

Some complained there were no night fighters, but on that night 121 were in the air. One German pilot described having to turn his bomber almost vertically over the city to avoid one. The great Douglas Bader and the war's greatest night-fighter pilot

Looking across Broadgate towards the first gutted Owen Owen store.

were over the city that night but made no contacts. The first effective night fighter radar-triangulation system had not then been introduced and in reality they were practically useless. This myth, like Enigma, has since been used to fuel the nonsense about Churchill sacrificing the city.

The tram system was destroyed as were 108 buses – seventy-three remained – and practically all gas and water pipes were smashed. Troops were brought in to clear the streets and the body parts that littered them. Rescue men, troops and the public worked day and night digging people out of the ruins. Ministry vans advised people where to get food and shelter. Canteens were set up and within three days electricity was restored; water and gas supplies returned shortly after. George VI visited on 16 November and on the 20th the first mass burial took place at the London Road Cemetery.

Raids continued. The Easter week raids of 8 April and 10 April 1941 were six and eight hours long. In the first raid the body of Christchurch was gutted. The last actual raid on Coventry was on 31 August 1942. The city had suffered forty-one actual raids, 371 siren alerts and 1,252 people were killed – some bodies were, however, never identified and some were never found.

Firemen tackling bombed-out Hertford Street.

The raids had a major impact on the city, described as one of the 'finest preserved medieval cities in Europe'. The destruction of the city centre especially hastened the already existing building plans that introduced Europe's first pedestrian precinct. Modern Coventry was created by bombs.

Blue Coat School

Blue Coat Charity School was founded around 1714 to educate poor girls – mainly orphans – and place them in service. Sermons at Holy Trinity and St Michael helped support it. In 1855, Blue Coat School Charity paid £275 to buy two empty houses and the original school in Priory Row. James Murray, a local architect, designed the new school in the fashionable Gothic style, intending it to be one of the most beautiful buildings in Coventry – it is! When clearing the site, the west entrance to the Priory

Blue Coat School stands on the entrance to the priory cathedral of St Mary. Beyond in the garden pillars of the building can be seen.

Cathedral of St Mary was discovered below. Work began in 1856 and was completed by public subscription the following year.

In 1859 it was stated

> FIFTY OF THE POOR GIRLS of this City are Educated in the Principles of the Church, and provided with Clothing and Books. The Six Senior Girls in succession are Boarded and Lodged for One Year in the School House, under the care of the Matron; and Instructed in the various Breaches of Domestic industry, such as Sewing, Washing, Cooking, etc...

In the twentieth century education was provided by the local authority and the school became a girls' orphanage. In 1940, the girls were evacuated and the building given over to the council, who gave it over to public transport workers. This continued until the early 1970s. From 1990 it stood empty until restored as part of the Council Phoenix Initiative.

Bond's Hospital

In 1497, Coventry draper and mayor Thomas Bond gave the Corporation property worth £49 11*s* 7*d* a year to create a Bede house at Bablake for ten poor men and one poor woman to attend them. A manuscript in the archives gives 1497 as the hospital's foundation date. Its other well-known foundation date is 1506, which is probably the date of its erection and first admissions as it would have taken time for rents to accumulate the money to build. Each pensioner was given a black hooded gown and a weekly pension.

The first inmates were required to attend matins, Mass, and evensong. The chaplain of Bond's looked after their spiritual needs and prayed for the souls of its founder, his father, grandfather, and all Christian souls. These houses were suppressed in 1547. But, after the city stating that suffering would ensue, the order was withdrawn and Bond's was granted to the mayor, bailiffs and commonalty at a rent of a penny a year.

In 1894, sixty received a 6*s* weekly pension, eighteen of whom were residents. They had two nurses caring for them, a common kitchen and sitting room. Two members of the council attended on Sundays when the roll was called and the almsmen paraded in their black hooded gowns to St John's.

The hospital faced the Bablake quadrangle, backed by the city wall. It was enlarged in 1816 to take extra inmates – one may have been John Johnson, an inmate who poisoned himself and several other inmates in 1819 and was buried in nearby crossroads. In 1832–34 it was extensively restored – some say rebuilt. Much original timber was reused. The carved window lintels are original, though the barge boards are copies. The lower windows are not in their original position and the chimneys – added later – were blown off in the war and rebuilt. In 1846–47 the Tudor-style Hill Street frontage was added. The building still fulfils its original purpose today.

Right: Bond's Hospital through the archway of Hill Street.

Below: Some inmates of Bond's photographed around 1905.

Inmates, Bonds Hospital, Coventry.

Castle

Coventry Castle was created around 1139 during the Barons' War by Ranulf Gernon, Earl of Chester. The original castle consisted of a motte and bailey with a wooden tower set within a ditched palisade. Marmion, Lord of Tamworth, had previously been promised the castle by Gernon, who changed his mind. In 1149, Marmion placed it under siege using St Mary's Church as his base. Marmion had mantraps dug between the structures. He rode out before Coventry Castle daily, then one day men burst forth taking him by surprise and in his hurry to escape Marmion fell into one of his own ditches and was decapitated by a common foot soldier.

Caesar's Tower painted by H. E. Cox in 1912 – currently in the Council House.

In 1145, Gernon was imprisoned by King Stephen, who ordered him to surrender his castles so Stephen acquired Coventry Castle. He was released in 1146 and rode on the castle laying it under siege. Gesta Stephani states, 'Also in front of the castle of Coventry, whither the King's men had withdrawn, the earl himself fortified a castle and valorously checked their sorties over the country until the King arrived escorted by a fine and numerous body of knights ... and fought a number of engagements with the earl...'

Gernon was seriously injured and put to flight, and the king laid siege to Gernon's siege castle, taking it and burning it to the ground. Coventry's wooden castle remained and was superseded by one built of stone, surrounded by three ditches and a stone keep. This castle stood around the area of St Mary's Hall. The 1160 charter of Gernon's son Hugh Keviloc mentions, 'the Broadgate of my castle' – hence Broadgate. In 1172, Hugh joined Robert of Leicester in rebellion against Henry II. Hugh lost the castle in 1173 and retook it in 1179. He died in 1181 and the castle was passed to his son Ranulf Blundeville. He mentions it the last time in 1199–1204 when he forbids his constables from bringing burgers to it to plead their causes. From this time the castle starts to run down.

In the mid-1100s the Langley Cartulary tells of the chapel of St Michael in the bailey, 'in ballivo', as it stood within the castle ditch. It also refers to Eustace fitz John granting property near the south gate; as there was no city wall, this must be the

A photograph taken during the clearance for the Council House. The original ancient Caesar's Tower stands out because of its whiteness.

castle's south gate. Eustace was later constable of Dover Castle. In the 1200s, on the Broadgate side, lived one Herman Att Castlegate.

Remnants of this castle have been unearthed in the now gone Derby Lane, Hay Lane, Bayley Lane and St Mary's Street, and also around and under the Guildhall. Caesar's Tower, at the rear of the hall, takes its name from a castle tower and probably began life as an entrance tower – originally four storeys with battlements and a turret. The original wedge-shaped tower before it was blown up in the war had massive post holes in the side to attach it to a second tower. Interestingly, the original tower was in ashler-grey sandstone, which looks white – a favoured colour choice for Norman military builders. This stone had to be brought in as Coventry sits on red sandstone. Much of the Guildhall itself is made up of robbed stone from the castle, creating a mix of red and white stone. Some of the larger stones from its base are now at the top of the great hall. At the rear of the hall was once a 6-foot-thick wall and at its side, outside the curtain wall, once stood the castle bakehouse.

Cars

Coventry once had the nickname 'Motor City' as it was the birthplace of the British motor car and was home to some of the greatest motor manufacturers in Britain, such as Daimler, Alvis, Humber, Armstrong-Siddeley, Riley, Singer, Standard, Triumph

Cars of the Great Horseless Carriage Company, 1897. In the car on the left at the tiller sits company manager Francis Baron; company cashier J. Barrows sits next to him. All except for one is an identifiable G. H. C. C. employee.

and Jaguar cars to name a few. The first British cars built here were in 1897 by the Great Horseless Carriage Co. in Draper's Field, Radford, at the Motor Mills factory shared with Daimler and Pennington cars. At this stage Daimler made engines but soon took over the GHHC in car production, becoming one of the country's most noted names.

Within a decade of the birth of the motor car, 10,000 were employed in the industry and by 1972 it had reached over 60,000. Jaguar began in the city as Swallow Sidecars, later becoming SS Cars, producing beautiful vehicles such as the SS100 at their Holbrooks/Whitmore Park works. At the outbreak of war the firm changed its name to Jaguar and later moved production to Browns Lane. Although no longer made in the city, Jaguar's design centre is in Whitley. Since 1896 there were 110 car manufacturers in the city; today the only surviving maker is LTI taxis. Recently, research into driverless cars has been taking place in Coventry, which still remains a centre of motor innovation.

Charterhouse Priory of Saint Anne

The Carthusians were one of the strictest monastic orders; they studied, laboured and kept conversation to 'talking days'. Charterhouse, named after the Chartreuse in France, was founded in 1381 by William Lord Zouch of Harringworth, who obtained

Exterior view of the Charterhouse with its prominent chimneys.

14 acres at Shortley on the edge of Coventry. Zouch nominated Richard II as the house's founder. He then got John Luscote (prior), Palmer the Procurator (the promoter of the idea), John Netherby (vicar of the house), and Edmund Balling, all from the Charter House in London to move here and they established themselves at a hermitage on the site. Later they were joined by seven others, creating the Coventry order.

Zouch left an endowment of £60 a year. His role was taken over by Richard Luffe (Mayor of Coventry), John Botoner, Adam Botoner (mayor in 1377 and 1385), and others. Luffe and John Botoner gave 400 marks towards building the church, cloisters and individual cells for the friars. In 1385, Richard II came with Queen Anne and laid the foundation stone. He also bestowed gifts of land and properties over his reign.

In 1398, Thomas Mowbray, Duke of Hereford, attended its church before the duel on Gosford Green. Nicholas of Hereford, friend of reformer John Wycliffe, who helped translate the Bible, died here in 1420. It was suppressed in 1539 and passed to Richard Andrews, gent, and Leonard Chamberleyn. The church was demolished in 1567 and the prior's lodgings and refectory converted into a private residence. In 1567, Henry Over, Coventry mercer, died here. It then passed through various hands including Robert Dudley, Earl of Leicester.

In 1848, John and Francis Wyley, wholesale chemists of Coventry, acquired it. Now in a dilapidated condition, the Wyleys repaired it and converted it into a double residence.

The Charterhouse's medieval crucifixion scene, showing Longinus as a knight.

Francis Wyley, councillor, alderman and mayor, occupied the southern half. Its best-known resident, Colonel Sir William Wyley, was responsible for converting it back into a single residence and uncovering the remarkable wall paintings, including the lower section of Christ crucified on the south wall, dating from around 1417. A councillor from 1876 to 1888, he was invited to become mayor in 1911 and 1912.

In his 1940 will Wyley left Charterhouse to the people of Coventry, wishing it to become a museum and park. The council rented it to numerous tenants, ending with Coventry City College. The college left in 2009 and in 2011 it was offered for sale. The Charterhouse Preservation Society was given possession in 2012. It is now part of the Historic Coventry Trust who finally recognised the building's rarity and international significance.

Cheylesmore Manor

Cheylesmore Gatehouse is all that remains of a moated royal residence built of stone and timber, with a gatehouse, courtyard, great hall and wings. Said to be built by the Earl of Arundel in 1230, in 1250 it was in the possession of Roger de Montalt and his wife, Cecily, who made a grant of Coventry to the monks of the priory in return for money granted to Roger for a journey to the Holy Land; however, they kept the manor for themselves and their heirs. The property eventually came to Queen Isabella, mother of Edward III. After her death Edward advanced his eldest son, Edward, the Black Prince, to the dukedom of Cornwall and settled the manor on him. The Prince stayed there on his way to Isabella's funeral. With the Prince's early death, it reverted to the Crown. Richard II had it encompassed by the city wall. At the beginning of the nineteenth century it and Cheylesmore Park – 'the Great Park' – was 3 miles in circumference and belonged to the Prince of Wales, inherited by him as Earl of Chester. It was later sold to the Marquis of Hertford.

In 1942, an engineering firm decided to knock down a row of old cottages with top shops adjoining the gatehouse. Tiles were pulled off and the ceiling ripped down, exposing a medieval timbered roof. Demolition was halted and the Ministry of Works recommended it be listed as an Ancient Monument. No one had realised that the cottages were part of the medieval hall, despite the medieval chimney at the end. The construction of the roof was considered a remarkable survival and still retained its original medieval tiles.

Even more remarkable is that this royal survivor didn't survive: it was demolished in 1956. The council didn't wish to save it as it was said to be unsafe and needed for 'necessary development'. The site lay untouched for over forty years. The surviving gatehouse was restored by the council in 1965. It is now the oldest register office in the country, consisting of a sixteenth-century gatehouse with two fourteenth-century wings. It was said that the manor house had a secret tunnel leading from its cellar; this was bricked up around 1900.

Cheylesmore Manor, *c.* 1896. Behind the gatehouse on the left is the surviving section of the hall.

The fine medieval roof of the hall before its demolition.

City Wall

Edward III gave the city the right to build a city wall; the first stone was laid at New Gate by Mayor Richard de Stoke in 1356. In 1364, Edward licensed a tax on traders and citizens to pay towards its building. As the southern section wasn't moving in 1384 the city petitioned Richard II to go forward with the work. The king gave licence as long as they enclosed his manor house at Cheylesmore and he also gave permission to cut stone from his quarry in Cheylesmore. In 1399, Richard gave a charter permitting the city to 'make improvements ... of all the gates, towers, walls ... about the town'.

In 1461 a section from Swanswell gate was rerouted as Prior Shotteswell complained it caused problems. Part of this new wall, including a corner round tower, was unearthed and reburied under student flats in 2017. This wall had enclosed the priory's stew pools and St Osburg's Pool. The finished wall included twelve gates – large and small – and thirty-two towers and measured nearly 2.5 miles around.

The walls were partly demolished in 1662 by order of Charles II as it had withheld his father in 1642. The city gates could have survived if it wasn't for a 1762 Act of Parliament passed for widening Coventry's streets. Under this five of the main gates were demolished by the Corporation, on the pretence that a loaded waggon couldn't pass through the arches – no one thought to bypass them. The last major gate to be demolished was Mill Lane Gate in 1849, leaving two minor gates: Swanswell and Cook Street Gate.

Swanswell Gate, also called Priory Gate, probably dates from the second half of the fourteenth century. It is often dated 1460, which is when Prior Shotteswell gained agreement to realign it. The actual wall was realigned below the gate with no need to rebuild the original gate. By 1820 the archway was partly blocked and the upper section turned into a weaver's shop. In 1852, it was blocked up and reroofed and in 1911 converted into a shop. Sir Alfred Herbert, who created Lady Herbert's Garden

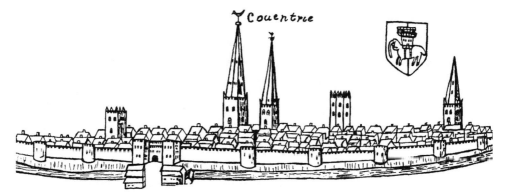

Copy of Smythe's view of walled Coventry from the north in 1576. The church towers are, from left to right: Whitefriars, St Michael, Holy Trinity, and the west main entrance of the priory and Greyfriars.

Above left: Swanswell Gate in Hales Street, taken from the Lady Herbert's garden.

Above right: Cook Street Gate was originally ditched and portcullissed.

as a memorial to his wife, Florence, gave it to the city in 1931 and in 1931–32 it was restored.

The other survivor, Cook Street Gate, is believed to have been built in the first quarter of the fourteenth century. It has a four-centred arch, side buttresses and restored battlements. Grooves show it once had a portcullis, as did all the gates. It is the oldest functioning gate in the city as it still straddles a road. It was purchased by Colonel Sir William Wyley who presented it to the city in 1913 as a public memorial. In a, 'dangerous' condition in 1916, it was restored by public funding in 1918. Both gates have recently been given over to the Historic Coventry Trust.

Coombe Abbey

The Cistercian abbey of Coombe was founded in 1150 by Richard de Camvill. In 1290, Edward I gave the abbot free range over his manors of Combe, Binley, Copston, Ernsford, Radbourn, Withybrook, and Wolvey. By 1291 it was the richest house in

24

Warwickshire; however, by 1332 it was in defective rule and given protection as a house of royal foundation and turned round with gifts from benefactors such as John de Pulteney of London. In 1345, Abbot Geoffrey was murdered here and Edward III ordered an inquiry with an impartial jury from Northamptonshire. The verdict is unknown, but Geoffrey still haunts the building. In 1451, Coombe was attacked on two days running by Sir Thomas Mallory (writer of *La Morte D'Arthur*) with 100 men who terrorised the monks and stole their money and valuables. In 1471, Edward IV spent a night here.

The abbey was surrendered in 1539 and went into royal hands in 1589. It was inherited by John Harrington of Exton who converted the main buildings into his home. In 1603, James I knighted Sir John and left his daughter, Princess Elizabeth, to be educated here at John's expense – it nearly bankrupted him. Part of the 1605 Gunpowder Plot was to forcibly take the princess from Coombe and set her up as a puppet monarch; however, she was brought into the safety of walled Coventry.

Coombe was acquired in 1622 by the Craven family, who enlarged it and added a west wing. They hired Capability Brown in 1771; he planted woodland and dammed the Smite, creating the great lake. The 6th Baron became the 1st Lord Craven in 1801. After the death of the last Lord Craven in 1921, the estate was sold. In 1923, John Gray, a builder, purchased the house and part of the estate. In wartime it housed the Royal Artillery and then GEC apprentices in the 1950s. In 1964, it was acquired by the council, who opened 150 acres as a country park. The house was restored by the council and the No Ordinary Hotels Group in 1992 and reopened as a hotel in 1995. It was purchased back by the council in 2017 for £11 million.

Coombe Abbey – set at the end of a mile-long lake.

Council House

Designed by Birmingham architects E. Garrett & H. W. Simister in 1911 to harmonise with St Mary's Hall and St Michael, its foundation stone was laid by Mayor William Wyley in June 1913. Work continued slowly because of the war, until it was completed in 1917. It was officially opened on 11 June 1920 by the Duke of York, later George VI. Garrett, who was killed in the war, failed to see its completion.

The heraldic shields in the central bay were designed by the architects in Runcorn sandstone – the same as the building. The first phase was completed for the opening of the Council House. The second, the Portland stone statues of Edward the Confessor, the Black Prince, Ranulf, Earl of Chester, Leofric, Godiva and Justice, were made shortly afterwards by Henry Wilson. Wilson was president of the Arts and Crafts Exhibition Society and was also responsible for the beautiful work in the Council Chamber reflecting the ancient Forest of Arden.

Wilson's figure of St Michael with a flaming sword astride a dragon on the handsome 100 foot clock tower dates from 1924. The building had all its windows smashed on 14 November 1940 and was peppered with shrapnel holes. These have nearly all been repaired over the years and since the removal of the modern bridge the building is now back to its original condition.

Above left: Coventry's Council House, a fine building decorated with some fascinating carvings.

Above right: Wilson's beautiful angel looks from the clock tower.

County Hall

County Hall was built on the site of the old Gaol Hall next to the gaol in 1783–84. Designed in classical style, it was an assizes court for the County and City of Coventry, which was abolished in 1842. Back under Warwickshire it was used for quarter sessions and weekly petty sessions for the Coventry district, and monthly sittings of the county court. Coventry Gaol, next door, was rebuilt and enlarged in 1772–73 and the governor's house in Pepper Lane was added in 1784. The gaol was closed in 1860 and demolished soon after.

The courtroom has windows in the upper level with fittings from the 1840s. Above the judge's chair is the original Georgian royal arms. Before its 1824 refit the courtroom was standing only; those involved in the trials mixed with the spectators and evidence was given from the front of the crowd. The accused stood in a spiked box in the centre of the room with steps down to the cells, which can still be seen.

Trials ranged from theft to murder. The condemned left the gaol via the Lodge Gate, right of the court entrance. They climbed aboard a cart with a clergyman and sat on their own coffin, praying as it trundled to the gallows on Whitley Common. The last on the cart was Mary Ann Higgins in 1831. Mary Ball, the last to hang in 1849, was hung from a drop gallows against the gaol wall, near the replica Coventry Cross. Her execution was attended by 30,000 people. She lies buried nearby.

In 1936, the council planned to demolish it under Gibson's rebuilding plan. In 1988, the courts were moved into Much Park Street. It stood empty for many years and is now a bar with the governor's house as valeted student apartments.

County Hall, centre of justice for nearly 200 years. The gaol's Lodge Gate stood on the right of the entrance.

Drapers' Hall

In 1424, it was enacted that no one sell cloth except at 'The Draperie', close to St Mary's Hall. By the end of the seventeenth century trade began to decline, and continued to do so into the eighteenth century as silk weaving became dominant.

The first hall erected by the Drapers' Company was in 1637. It was considered dark and gloomy so was taken down in 1775 and replaced by a classic-style building, which was condemned with dry rot in 1829. The present hall was designed in the Greek revival style and opened in 1832. It originally had no windows, relying on skylights. In 1890, architect E. Burgess added the brick extension and removed the two right-hand columns of the portico and inserted a window.

The ballroom remains unchanged with many original features, such as the musician's gallery, fireplaces and gilded mirrors. It has a beautiful ceiling with decorative mouldings in the Greek style. The ballroom was used as a lecture room and venue for balls, dinners, plays and concerts throughout the nineteenth and twentieth centuries.

In October 1939 the drapers and council were discussing its demolition. It may have been saved by the fact that in the same year the cellar became a public air-raid shelter.

Interior of Drapers' Hall showing the fine ballroom.

Drapers' has been uncared for since the Second World War, various ideas have come to nothing; but its future hopefully looks brighter under the Historic Coventry Trust.

Duel on Gosford Green

The duel on Gosford Green is usually placed in 1397, but this date is incorrect. On 29 September 1397 Henry Bolingbroke was created Duke of Hereford, and Thomas Mowbray, Duke of Norfolk. Shortly after, the men accused each other of uttering treasonable words against the king and appeared at Shrewsbury Parliament, which ran between 27 and 30 January 1398. Here Hereford repeated his charges against Mowbray. On 4 February 1398 a summons was issued to Norfolk to appear before the king and on 23 February 1398 both men appeared before Richard II at Oswestry and the matter was referred to the Court of Chivalry, led by the king at Windsor.

This court ordered on 29 April 1398 that the dispute should be settled by combat at Coventry on 16 September 1398. The king attended with 10,000 armoured men and called a halt to proceeding during the first charge. The men were banished and Richard granted Hereford the right to remain at Sandgate Castle for six weeks. He seems to have left England by 13 October 1398. This event was a turning point in national history as later Bolingbroke returned, usurped Richard and took the throne as Henry IV. The fact that it took place on Gosford Green is a detail added in the eighteenth century, but is, however, very likely correct.

A Victorian image of the duel between Bolingbroke and Mowbray on Gosford Green.

Eliot, George

George Eliot was literally born in Coventry, and if she hadn't come to the city she would never have become the famed novelist we know today. Mary Ann Evans (her real name) was in Coventry from 1832–36 to finalise her education at the school of the Franklin sisters at No. 29 Warwick Row. At this time her religious zeal would have made her a good vicar's wife. She came back in March 1841 when her father, Robert Evans, retired to Bird Grove, a Georgian house in rural Foleshill. She lived here for eight years, starting her literary career in her small study – this still exists today. Here for two years, she translated Strauss's *Life of Christ* while looking through the small window at the three spires.

George Eliot, 1864.

Her new neighbours, Abijah and Elizabeth Pears, introduced her to Elizabeth's brother, Charles Bray, and his wife Caroline and her sister Sarah Hennell at Rosehill on the Radford Road. It was this meeting with the freethinking Brays and their wide circle of intellectual friends that led to the creation of 'George Eliot' as we know her today. At this time her reversal in thinking led to her refusal to attend Holy Trinity. Her father, a plate bearer there, sent her away for four months until the Brays and Pears convinced him to let her return.

Bray, a social reformer, bought the *Coventry Herald* as his political mouthpiece and while at Bird Grove Mary Ann wrote her first works for Bray's *Herald*. One called 'Vice and Sausages', published in 1847, was a satire on Coventry's Chief Constable John Vice and a scandal involving Coventry butchers.

Robert Evans died at Bird Grove in 1849. Mary Ann went to the Continent with the Brays and shortly after moved into Rosehill. While there she was invited to write for the *Westminster Review* and moved to London. Mary Ann kept in touch with her beloved 'eternal triangle' of Coventry friends and in 1857 her first novel, *Scenes of Clerical Life*, was published ... the rest is history.

Rural Bird Grove as it appeared in her time. Half of the building is now gone and is encompassed by housing. Her study window is above the door on the right.

First British Aeroplane

Humber Ltd from Coventry built the first all-British aeroplane in 1909. Everything about the machine was British, even the measurements, and all 400 parts were made at the Humber Works, which at that time stood isolated in the fields. The general manager at the time was H. G. Burford, a noted engineer who built these planes with around 200 men under another notable engineer, Captain Lovelace, formerly chief mechanic to the famous Wright Brothers.

The length of the monoplane was 28 feet 9 inches and 25 feet wide. The engine was an adapted Humber engine, with three engines set in a quarter circle, giving around 30 hp.

Not the first aeroplane but the first Daimler aeroplane to leave Radford aerodrome in the First World War.

Ford's Hospital

Ford's, also known as Greyfriars Hospital, is considered one of the finest examples of sixteenth-century architecture in England. It was founded in 1509 as an almshouse for five men with one woman to attend them under the will of Coventry merchant William Ford. It was enlarged in 1517 by Ford's executor, William Pisford, to six poor men and their wives, and later in the eighteenth century and for most of its modern history it was home for fifteen elderly women. The building originally had a chapel over the entrance, the chaplain having his own room tended the inmates and said Mass for the soul of William Pisford.

Ford's took a direct hit from a high explosive on 14 October 1940; the section near the front was partly wrecked, killing the matron and eight inmates. The courtyard escaped serious damage as the oak framing absorbed much of the blast. In 1941, it was proposed to move it elsewhere to accommodate Gibson's new development. It, however, remained and was restored, reopening in 1953.

View of the beautiful courtyard of Ford's Hospital.

Giant's Grave

This ancient tumulus stood in Primrose Hill Park until the beginning of the twentieth century, near the bandstand. It was around 8 feet high and egg-shaped, like the tumulus at Uley in Gloucestershire. Despite quarrying in the past it was left untouched, but during building work here the burial mound got buried. Apparently, the ground had to be made up for the west side of Nicholls Street when the houses were built, the trees were felled on the tumulus and it was buried beneath hundreds of tons of soil, which formed the back gardens of the houses. No attempt was made to excavate it until the late twentieth century when archaeologists dug another nearby mound assuming it was the Giant's Grave, but it was a spoil heap from the building work. Sadly, the significant, real, Giant's Grave (probably Neolithic and dating before 3000 BC) still lies buried under nearby gardens.

There were – and are – numerous prehistoric sites in and around Coventry: two bronze axe heads dating to 350 BC were buried in Broadgate, and there are burial mounds in St Michael's Churchyard, Radford, Cheylesmore, Whitley Common and Coombe. The area from Warwick University into Earlsdon has numerous

The Giant's Grave, 1910.

prehistoric sites. The university site was once a massive Iron Age village and there was a hill fort in Whitley and Barrs Hill, Radford. Beyond in Keresley, sites dating from the Neolithic back to the Mesolithic await obliteration by planned housing.

Gill, William 'Paddy'

William 'Paddy' Gill, Coventry's greatest prize fighter, fought his first notable fight with Young Foster in Leicestershire, defeating him in fifty-seven rounds, taking two hours and twelve minutes. His second victory was against Tom Pritchard on Stoke Heath in 1843. He then fought Bill Hubbard at Griff Hollows; the fight was broken up by constables and refought two weeks later – Gill won in forty-two rounds.

In June 1843 he beat Ned Bentley, walking away practically untouched, but leaving Bentley in a 'fearful state'. In October he hit the big league, taking on George Norley for £100. Lasting sixty-six rounds it was Gill's first defeat, caused mainly by a severely injured leg when he was thrown onto a ring stake. He next defeated Jack Bethell of Birmingham for £100, then beat George Holden of Walsall.

He took on and defeated Young Reed outside Oxford in 1845 and in November he was matched again against Norley for £200 a side. This failed to take place as Gill was arrested. It did, however, take place for £500 the following year at Witney, lasting an incredible four hours and seven minutes and 160 rounds before a crowd of thousands – Gill was victorious. The following year he took on the Lamb & Flag and announced his retirement.

Paddy Gill in his heyday.

A typical prize fight from Paddy's time.

Having an account to settle he met Tom Maley in 1848, winning £200 after two and a half hours. He then beat Tom Griffiths in 1850 for £280 in sixty-three rounds at Frimley Green. Griffiths died after the match ended. Gill was arrested and tried at the Kingston Assizes in March 1851. He was acquitted as witnesses refused to identify him. Paddy lost his heart in the game and was defeated in his last fight against M'Nulty in 1854. He retired and for several years kept the Lamp Tavern in the market square.

A benefit was held for him at the Theatre Royal in 1863, but three months before his death his mind gave way and he was put in Hatton Lunatic Asylum. Here he died on 19 October 1869, aged fifty. Bell's Life said of him, 'We never saw a man possessed of better milling qualities, or one whom we consider more entitled to the rank of Champion of the Light Weights.' Paddy was buried in London Road Cemetery and although his burial place was looked after in the past it is now unmarked.

Godiva

Godiva was one of the most powerful women in England. Her original name was Godgifu, meaning, 'God's Gift'. She was born around 1000 and her brother was probably Thorold, Sheriff of Lincolnshire. She was described by the chronicler Ingulphus as 'the most beauteous of all women of her time'. That said, he never saw her, for no chronicler talks of Godiva until nearly 200 years after her death when her legendary ride was first recorded.

Godiva owned land in six counties; her largest holding was in Newark, Nottinghamshire. It is believed that she married twice and was widowed in approximately 1028, around the time she suffered a life-threatening illness. During this period she made bequests to Ely church to ensure her place in Heaven. This close call with death left its mark and she became deeply religious and devoted to the Virgin.

Lady Godiva as painted by Jules Lefebvre, 1907.

She later gave many of her jewels to Coventry's abbey church to be converted into crosses etc., and she left her jewelled gold necklace to hang on the church's image of the Virgin.

A common mistake concerning Godiva is that she lived and was buried in Coventry – both are untrue. Godiva and Leofric's residence was at King's Bromley in Staffordshire. Leofric died there. Leofric and their son Aelfgar are, however, buried in Coventry. Godiva was around fifty-seven when Leofric died, her son Aelfgar then inherited the Mercian earldom and she went into retirement.

She may later have gone into a religious house, it was quite normal at the time for widowed noblewomen to live in such houses or even become a nun. Godiva appears to have spent time at Evesham Abbey, where she and Leofric built the Church of Holy Trinity. She chose Evesham because Prior Aefic, her Father Confessor, resided there. This Benedictine monk, the Evesham Chroniclers claim, convinced Godiva to found a new Benedictine house of monks in Coventry.

It is noted that Godiva attended the funeral of Aefic at Trinity and the Evesham Chronicle states she was later buried there, saying,

> Then your worthy Prior Aefic departed from this daylight in the year of Our Lord's Incarnation one thousand and thirty-eight, and his grave worthily exists in the same church of the Blessed Trinity near that of the same pious Countess Godiva, and of whom, so long as he lived, he was a friend.

This is the only source relating to her burial, apart from later chroniclers assuming it was Coventry. The only source we have for her death is the Douce Manuscript at Oxford, which states she died on 10 September 1067.

Ann Wrigg as Lady Godiva in 1952.

The first reference to her ride doesn't appear until 1190 when told to Roger of Wendover by displaced monks from Coventry Priory. The original tale is a miraculous one: the people complain about bondage to Leofric and Godiva rides naked through the marketplace from end to end where all are assembled but nobody sees her. Leofric proclaims it a miracle and drops their servitude. A later version drops the miracle and Godiva is shielded in it by her hair rather than God. The tale is still changed to this day. The story probably originated with ancient fertility rituals. In 1678, Godiva (a boy called Swinnerton) rode before the mayor and corporation and companies to proclaim the Great Fair, and thereafter many have ridden as Godiva in the city.

Greyfriars

Founded by St Francis of Assisi, the monastic order arrived in Coventry in 1234 and built their church and friary on land given by Ranulf, Earl of Chester. They were sworn to poverty and survived purely on charity. In 1358, William Galeys founded a chantry here for three priests and a warden, and built a chapel in honour of the Virgin. The priests celebrated Mass for the good estate of Edward III, Queen Isabella (his mother), Edward, Prince of Wales, and for Galeys himself. Sir Roger Mortimer, Marcher Lord, lover of Queen Isabella, was buried here, as were other nobles, for to be buried in the robes of a Greyfriar ensured entrance to Heaven.

Edward, the Black Prince, allowed them to take stone from his quarry in the Great Park and the Hastings family of Allesley and Fillongley Castles were benefactors and interned in its Hastings Chapel. As their influence waned so did their income and at the Dissolution of the Monasteries their house was dilapidated.

Eleven friars signed the suppression order in 1538, giving it to the king. It was then granted to the mayor, bailiffs and commonalty of Coventry. After its destruction stone was taken to repair the city walls. Greyfriars' tower and spire (the smallest of Coventry's three spires) survived and in the early eighteenth century was used by Mr Seagar as a pigsty – he boasted it was the tallest pigsty in the kingdom.

The original church was cruciform with a central octagonal tower. In 1826 the Commission of Parliamentary Grants for Building Churches said if the inhabitants would raise half of the sum to rebuild they would pay the rest. Work began on the new church – now Christchurch – in 1829 and it was consecrated in 1832. Inside it was 101 feet long with side aisles and six Perpendicular windows each side, and a round window over the altar. This second church was destroyed by bombs on 8 April 1941, once again leaving the tower and spire standing alone. It is now a café and currently being dwarfed by a splash centre.

Griffiths Delin. *Lodge Sculpt.*
View of GREYFRIERS GATE *and* STEEPLE, *in the*
City *of* Coventry *in* Warwickshire .

Greyfriars Tower next to Greyfriars Gate in 1782.

Holy Trinity

Holy Trinity was originally attached to Coventry Priory and used to free up the Benedictine cathedral to the bishop, prior, monks and pilgrims. It is thought Trinity was erected between 1101 and 1113 and was first documented in 1139. It may, however, have begun life as a Saxon minster; its cruciform shape shows high status. Significantly, the Cathedral of St Mary was not built in the parish of St Mary but the parish of Holy Trinity. The proximity of chapels in the twelfth century suggests the presence of a minster church. Curfew bells rang from mother churches, Coventry's rang from Trinity. Fair days were fixed on the day of the main church's dedication; Coventry's Great Fair Day was fixed in 1218 on the festival of the Holy Trinity. Early charters refer to St Mary's, St Michael and 'the parish church' – this can only be Holy Trinity. All suggestive that Trinity was originally a minster, the mother church of Coventry.

Believed to have been destroyed by fire in 1257 and rebuilt, the original chancel is thought to have survived and in 1391 was 'ruinated and decayed'. This is likely to be part of a much older building. By the late fourteenth century it began its association

Holy Trinity Church – its parish predated the priory.

with guilds, who set up altars inside. In 1392, the merchant Corpus Christi Guild paid a priest to sing Mass five times a day for its members, King Richard II and Queen Anne. Trade guilds followed: in 1517 the butchers created a chapel, followed by the dyers and tanners. Chantry chapels came, the first being Cellet's or the Jesus Chapel.

The Marler Chapel was built last in 1526 willed by Richard Marler, one of England's wealthiest merchants. Beneath lays a rare, untouched charnel house. In 1522, the church had eleven priests, two chantry priests, a vicar, a high altar and at least eight other altars around the building. Trinity lost eight priests in the Dissolution and by 1560 the rood screen and high altar had gone, replaced by a Protestant Communion table.

The doom painting over the chancel arch was created in 1435–60, probably prompted by an earthquake. It shows the dead rising from their graves and being judged by Christ. On the left is St Peter at the gates of Heaven and on the right is the mouth of Hell. It was originally whitewashed out by reformers, but was partially visible from the late eighteenth century. In 1831, local artist David Gee was paid £25 to restore it. Gee protected it with a coat of megilp, which over time went black. Add to this the smoke from oil lamps and by the 1860s the image began to disappear. In 2002 work began on restoration; the actual cleaning took a year. This restoration of the doom painting gave Coventry and the nation a new treasure.

Inside Trinity. Above the chancel arch is one of the finest doom paintings in England.

Inquest

The earliest recorded inquest or trial for witchcraft in England is recorded in Coventry when Robert de Sowe was killed in 1325 by magic. John de Nottingham, a necromancer who lived near the Charterhouse, was hired by a number of local gentry to kill Edward II, the Bishop of Coventry and others by witchcraft. Nottingham killed Sowe by using a wax figure and pins to prove his art. During the inquest Nottingham was held by the marshal, Robert de Dumbleton, but he failed to testify after he suddenly died in captivity so the inquest ended and the gentry walked free.

Edward II, the ultimate
target of the Coventry plot.

J

Judge

Coventry's most notable judge and three times mayor was Alderman John Hewitt. On taking on the mayoralty in 1755 he swore an oath to fight crime and became Coventry's greatest thief taker, becoming a personal friend of noted London thief takers Sir John and Henry Fielding. One of his early cases involves the Coventry Gang, who were part of a notorious 200-strong London gang. Hewitt had four of its members hanged in Coventry and destroyed the entire gang over his career. He also tracked down and hung the murders of Stoneleigh farmer Thomas Edwards in 1765. Their execution and gibbeting is remembered today by local landmark Gibbet Hill. It was not unusual to find Hewitt, sometimes alone, smashing down the doors of criminals during the night. Those who hung on Gibbet Hill said they would die happy if they could blow out his brains!

Hewitt is also remembered for the huge feast he held in St Mary's Hall in 1755, his gentlemanly behaviour and high regard for the protection of Coventrians and the comfort of ladies. He lies buried today somewhere in the south aisle of Holy Trinity Church.

Alderman John Hewitt's handwriting in an unpublished section of his eighteenth-century journal.

Keane, F. W.

F. W. Keane was the early stage name of Ira Aldridge, a black American made manager, in February 1828, by my four times great-uncle Sir Skears Rew of his theatre, the Theatre Royal in Smithford Street (not the Coventry Theatre as stated on a plaque by the old British Home Stores).

   Son of a pastor, he left America after his first performances caused a riot. His father sent him to England to study theology but the acting bug bit again. He was a celebrated talent and played *Othello*, *Macbeth* and *Shylock*; he was also noted for his comedy rolls. His play *The Slave* performed at the Theatre Royal in 1828 got people talking about slavery. Although Coventry already had a history of anti-slavery for in 1823, 1824 and 1831 the city petitioned Parliament against it. Aldridge later got the nickname the 'African Roscius'. He had left Coventry by 1830 and toured in many countries, dying in Poland.

Above: Sir Skears Rew built the first official theatre in Coventry. His portrait is in St Mary's Hall.

Left: Ira Aldridge, twenty years after he left Coventry.

L

Leofric

Leofric, Earl of Mercia, was the third son of Leofwine, Ealdorman of the Hwicce. He succeeded his father around 1024. He was King Canute's close and trusted friend and in 1026 Canute made him 'hlaford Mrycena' (Lord of the Mercians), one of the three most powerful men in the land. Canute had two sons, Harold and Hardicanute. Leofric assisted Harold to the throne in 1035 and helped Hardicanute suppress a revolt in Worcestershire. When Edward the Confessor came to power, Godwin, Earl of Wessex, assembled an army against him and Leofric and Siward, Earl of Northumbria, defended the king, driving Godwin into exile.

The Anglo-Saxon Chronicle states he was 'wise for God and for the world'. Many thought him a saint and with King Edward he saw a vision of Christ in the Chapel of Our Lady at Westminster. He owned tracts of land in Staffordshire and Warwickshire and effectively controlled England from the east coast to the Welsh Marches.

Godiva and Leofric were married around 1028. Leofric founded a Benedictine house of monks in Coventry, replacing the nuns of St Osburg's, which had been attacked by the Danes in 1016. This was in accordance with the wishes of Godiva's father confessor.

The black eagle attributed to Leofric in the north window of St Mary's Hall.

The silver crowned eagle of Mercia, one of two above the north window.

There was an abbot and twenty-four monks and it was dedicated to the Virgin Mary, St Peter, St Osburg and All Saints by Edsi, Archbishop of Canterbury. During the dedication ceremony, Leofric laid the charter on the altar, granting lordship over twenty-four villages for its maintenance. Leofric died at his home in King's Bromley, Staffordshire, on 30 October 1057 and the Anglo-Saxon Chronicle records: 'He was very wise in all matters, both religious and secular, that benefitted all this nation.' His body was brought to his Coventry church with a gift of gold and silver and he was laid to rest in one of its porches.

History tells us that Leofric's symbol is the black eagle, but is this true? Basically, early history doesn't mention Leofric's eagle – heraldry didn't appear until the twelfth century. It is generally assumed that it got linked to Leofric because in the 1700s a tile decorated with a cream-coloured eagle was found in the priory, but why is Leofric associated with the black eagle? One clue may be Sir William Dugdale's *History and Antiquities of Warwickshire*, published in 1656, in which he identifies the black eagle in the King's Window in St Mary's Hall as Leofric's eagle. This, however, appears to be incorrect, for if one looks at Constantine's surcoat in the same window, the identical black eagle can be seen – this is Constantine's eagle, not Leofric's. Dugdale's misidentification either started or continued the belief. If Leofric was to have a device as Earl of Mercia it should represent the kingdom of Mercia, which is the double-headed silver eagle with crown seen in the ceiling of St Mary's Hall.

Lych Gate Cottages

Lych Gate Cottages bear a plaque that claims they were built as part of the forecourt of Coventry Priory in the spring of 1415, a date based on six test samples. Traditionally, they are known to have been built from reused timbers and stand on brick barrel-vaulted cellars, which appear to be seventeenth century. Also, the ground floor of the building stands nearly 14 feet higher than the ground level of the priory forecourt behind. It stands on the edge of the west tower, which was demolished in 1648. It also makes little sense having timbered domestic houses on the forecourt as the area was originally secure with a wall and gatehouse.

The Trinity Deeds of 1650 make it clear when and who built them, stating:

> Whereas the west part of the ruins of the Cathedral Church of St. Mary, in this city, that was demolished in the reign of Henry VIII had been made use of by butchers to keep hogs in, the city this year gave to Mr. John Bryan, Vicar of Trinity, a grant thereof from the City, and built a dwelling House [for himself called Tower House] over against the Lane, between the two Churchyards, where formerly a steeple stood belonging to the said Cathedral, the Cross Iles going over there. He also made dwelling Houses on the Bottom of the two steeples that were on both sides of the Entrance into the Priory, from the Butcherow, and cleansed the ground of the ruins, and converted it to Gardens.

Bryan seemed to have reused old timbers, possibly from the priory or more likely out of the churchyard for the Holy Trinity Churchwardens Account for 1644 prove they were there. It reads, 'Payments for taking downe diverse houses and buildings without Bishop's gate and Spon gate ... and bringing the tiles and Timber into Trinitie Church.' No doubt some came from a building dating 1415. Other buildings were rebuilt in nearby New Buildings. The cottages were private houses through the centuries. They were acquired by the council in 1937 and restored in 1997–98. In 2017 they were passed to the Historic Coventry Trust.

Lych Gate Cottages in Priory Row.

Martyrs

It was said Coventry was a 'special nest of heresy'. It has contributed its quota of martyrs who were burnt at the stake, among them Robert Glover and Cornelius Bongey, both burned alive together in the Great Park on 19 September 1555. Foxe's Book of Martyrs tells us of these men, both were men of principle and learning. Cornelius Bongey was not as well known as Robert Glover. He was a capper and the charge against him was that for three years 'in the city of Coventry and places thereabout, he did hold, maintain, argue and teach certain doctrines held to be heretical'.

Glover was educated at Eaton and Cambridge, a gentleman, and at the time of his arrest was living with his brother at Mancetter; he was actually arrested in place of his missing brother, while ill in bed and held in Coventry, awaiting the convenience of the bishop. Glover wouldn't change his beliefs and was condemned to be burned at the stake in the Coventry Park. He may have been held in the undercroft of St Mary's Hall as he wrote this letter:

> The second day after the bishop's coming to Coventry; Master Warren came to the Guildhall, and willed the chief jailer to carry me to the bishop. I laid to Master Warren's charge the cruel seeking of my death; and when he would have excused himself, I told him he could not wipe his hands so; he was as guilty of my blood before God, as though he had murdered me with his own hands.

Interestingly, the heavy wooden door from the kitchen in the undercroft has an opening so one can look inside. It also has unusually shaped bars with a gap to pass food through.

Other Coventry martyrs were Joan Ward, Alice Lansdail, Thomas Lansdail, Hosea Hawkins, Thomas Wrexham, Lawrence Saunders, John Careless, Robert Hockett, Thomas Bond and Robert Silksby – all murdered in the name of religion.

The Martyrs' Memorial at the end of Little Park Street originally stood adjacent the place of the burnings. It was unveiled in 1910. There is also a mosaic commemorating them in Broadgate House.

Above left: The 'purification' of Robert Glover and Cornelius Bongey. My eight-times great-uncle, Francis Kett, was purified at Norwich Castle.

Above right: All those martyred passed through Little Park Gate at the end of Little Park Street on their way to the Park Hollows, a sandpit where their destruction took place.

Mint

The oldest coin found on the *Mary Rose* was a gold ryal, struck in Coventry's Royal Mint between 1465 and 1467. This mint was set up by Edward IV during his national recoinage on 6 July 1465. No document says where it was but tradition says it stood on the site of the Golden Cross on the corner of Hay Lane. The only historian who mentions it is Leland, who said, 'There was a Parliament and a Mint of coynage at Coventry.' There are, however, gold and silver coins from the reign of Edward IV bearing the 'C' of the Coventry mint under the king's head and the words, 'Civitas Coventre'.

References to the tradition that the Cross was the site can be found from the beginning of the nineteenth century. The original inn wasn't called the Golden Cross, it was probably the Royal Exchange mentioned here in 1693. Its existence probably left us with the tradition, for exchanges also housed mints. Coventry's mint and exchange in 1465 was under the control of Hugh Boyce. The Cross itself was the Dog and Duck in 1756, and in 1770 it was the Cross Guns. The earliest mention of the Golden Cross name is in 1818.

The Golden Cross, built on the site of the old mint.

A drawing of a silver Coventry groat – a 4*d* piece.

N

Name

The name Coventry has often been claimed as 'Cofantreo'. This was first put forward in 1890. That actual word only appears once and not as the earliest spelling. The translation is problematic as Cofan or Cofa isn't a personal name; it refers to the heart and is used singularly.

'Couaentree' is the earliest spelling; the first part of the word comes from 'Couaen,' or 'Cune'. Cune is the ancient name for the Sherbourne. The 'tree' or 'treabh' is a farmed settlement, so the name means 'settlement by the Cune'. The Cune/Sherbourne rises from the ground, making it a sacred river to ancient people. It travels through Coundon, the eminence by the Cune, then to Coventry. The later Saxon title 'Sherbourne' means 'shining stream', the 'shining' again implies a sacred water. Cune is also associated with a sacred meeting place of waters, a description that certainly fits the centre of Coventry with its now lost lake, river and streams that met here. Where the Og meets the Kennet in southern England the Romano-British called it 'Cunetio'. There is also a 'Cound' meeting the Severn. These were sacred to the Celtic god Coundatis, the god associated with the meeting of waters. I believe the origin of Coventry's name lies here.

The spring-fed Sherbourne in Palmer Lane. In the seventeenth century there were trout here.

Old Grammar School

St John's Hospital it is said to have been founded around 1157 by Prior Laurence of St Mary's Priory. It is said he gave the land and it was constructed under direction of Edmund, Archdeacon of Coventry. Interestingly, this hospital/church came under the Order of the Knights of the Hospital of St John of Jerusalem, the Knights Hospitallers. Founded in 1023, the order cared for sick and injured pilgrims in Jerusalem and became a military fighting order. Strangely, at the time of St John's foundation the Hospitallers were not favoured by the Benedictines. The Hospitallers later inherited the estates of the purged Knights Templar, making it possible the building had a different origin, itself purged from history.

It had three priests in 1522, three clerks and five sisters and maintained thirty beds. Part of the chancel and choir were reserved for religious purposes, while beds for the

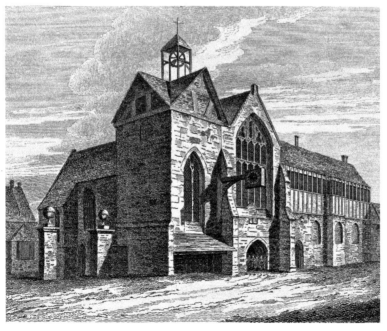

An engraving of the Old Grammar School. The half-timbered section housed the library, among other things. This section was demolished with the laying out of Hales Street in the 1840s. A legend attached to this building, which may link to the Templars, is that men supposedly raised the Devil here using magic.

sick and infirm lined the walls of the rest of the chancel and nave. The present building was the church and the original complex included infirmary, hall and lodgings. Much is thought to have been rebuilt in the early 1300s.

Surrendered in 1544, it was granted to John Hales in 1546. Hales, one the king's commissioners in the dissolution of Coventry's monastic houses, acquired the hospital and part of Whitefriars. Henry VIII gave them on the condition he set up a grammar school in the city. Hales set up the school in the choir of Whitefriars church, which belonged to the Corporation and was made to remove it. He then moved it to St John's and with it went some choir stalls as desks.

In 1628 the first recorded rules were made:

> ...for the teaching of grammar and musick unto the children of all the Free Inhabitants within this Citie and the inner liberties thereof, and to none other ... All other Fforyners coming thither shall compound with the Maister and the Usher for theire teaching.

It closed in 1885 and the pupils moved to Henry VIII School, a majestic building in Warwick Road. In that year the old building was threatened with demolition but saved by Canon Beaumont of Holy Trinity. In 1941, it received minor bomb damage and in 1952 the council requested its demolition to widen Bishop Street, but the Ministry of Works refused. For many years it stood empty, and from 2012 it was designated at risk. In 2013, as part of a lottery bid, Trinity Church and the Transport Museum received £1.5 million to restore it on the condition it became more publically accessible – as yet, it hasn't.

Inside the Grammar School today, which remains relatively unchanged since it opened.

Parkes, Sir Henry

Henry Parkes was born in 1815 at Moat House Cottage, Canley, then on the Stoneleigh estate. His family had been tenant farmers there for nearly a century. Not long after his birth his father, Thomas, moved the family to a larger farm near Gibbet Hill. Henry and his six siblings grew up on this farm and attended Stoneleigh village school.

In 1822, his father had an accident, making it difficult for him to run the farm. At the same time his rent rose and by 1823 he was in debt and lost the farm. From this time the family struggled, and by the age of eleven Henry was working in a Birmingham rope factory. He later joined a rock-breaking gang and when twelve years old was apprenticed to a bone and ivory turner. He began to self-educate, joined the Birmingham Mechanics' Institute and at sixteen became fascinated by politics, such as the Chartist movement.

Sir Henry Parkes.

In 1839 he and his young wife Clarinda set off for New South Wales, their first child was born aboard two days before they reached Sydney. Henry set about finding work and eventually in 1850 founded a newspaper called *The Empire*. He ultimately became a politician and was known as 'Father of the Federation'. Parkes was elected Premier of New South Wales five times and is remembered today for his contribution to Australian politics. The town of Parkes was named after him and twinned with Coventry and his image now appears on Australian banknotes and coins.

Parkes, John

John Parkes of Coventry, known as the 'Invincible', was a professional duellist of great renown. These Gladiators, as they were known, were the forerunners of the boxers of today. In fact, Parkes' great friend was the renowned James Fig, the acknowledged sword master and boxer of the age. He was described as accurate and deadly and bore few scars – unlike his opponents.

To give some idea of the science that Parkes was an exponent of, the following challenge gives some idea:

> The Bear Garden in Hockley-in-the-Hole. A Tryal of Skill to be Performed between these two following Masters of the Noble Science of Defence, on Wednesday the Fifth of April, 1710, at Three of the Clock, precisely John Parkes, from Coventry, Master of the Noble Science of Defence, do Invite you, Thomas Hesgate, to meet me, and Exercise at these following weapons, viz.: Back Sword, Sword and Dagger, Sword and Buckler, Single Falchion. Case of Falchions and quarterstaff. I Thomas Hesgate, a Barkshire Man. Master of the said Science, will not fail (God Willing) to meet this brave and bold Inviter at the Time and Place appointed; desiring Sharp Swords, and from him no Favour. Note, no person to be upon the Stage but the Seconds. Vivat Regina.

The grave of John Parkes in St Michael's Avenue, the third stone on this site.

Parkes also fought the noted James Millar in a display of sword fighting and tilting at Fig's great tilt booth on the bowling green in 1711. Parkes shared equal honours with James Fig, James Millar, and Timothy Buck as national sporting heroes of the early eighteenth century. He died – nationally mourned – in 1733, after having fought 350 armed combats throughout Europe.

Peeping Tom

Peeping Tom is famous throughout the world as the tailor who peeped through the shutters at Lady Godiva. Tom does not belong to the original story of Godiva; he is a newcomer from the seventeenth century, being based on Greek mythology as the voyeur who looks upon the naked goddess and is struck blind. His earliest mention is when John Warren wrote: 'Beeing in Couentry in the year 1659, and at the end of the stret going to the Cross, out of the window stands a statu of a man. I asked one of the cittezens what it ment [and he] related this story [of Godiva].' It is usually assumed Tom was added in during the Restoration but this entry is from the last days of the Commonwealth, so Tom is a little older than thought.

The figure that Warren talks of is the figure of Tom we still have today, which dates from the fifteenth century and is believed to have originally been a representation of St George, who legend says was born in Caludon Castle and died in Coventry. This figure has been used since the seventeenth century to represent Tom and for many years had its own nook in the King's Head Hotel. Tom was removed from the King's Head as it burned on the night of the Big Raid. He now stands in Cathedral Lanes.

Tom, photographed by Wingrave in the 1860s, being prepared to peep at the Godiva procession from his nook in the King's Head. He was often repainted for the rides and wore his tin plumed hat.

Precinct

Designed by Donald Gibson, Coventry's Precinct was the first pedestrian precinct in Europe. Built in Festival of Britain style, the first building formed the corner of the Upper Precinct and facing Broadgate was Broadgate House. Opened in 1953 it was built on council land and cost £400,000; it still contains council offices and shops. It also originally bridged Hertford Street, keeping an open flow from Broadgate, but sadly this was filled but planned to be reopened.

It was followed by the Hotel Leofric, designed by Coventry architect Hattrells and opened in 1955, forming the other corner. It was the finest hotel in the city centre and is now student accommodation. The buildings that followed formed the upper and lower two-tiered precincts, half almost follows the line of pre-war Smithford Street and was inspired by the Rows in Chester. This is crossed by Smithford and Market Way. At the crossroads M&S, BHS and Woolworths were built. Gibson left in 1955 and work continued under Arthur Ling. Ling wanted more height and added blocks of flats. The lines of Gibson's work were originally more flowing and took perspectives into account; some of this has been affected by modern additions.

Looking up the Upper Precinct towards Broadgate, 1960s.

Looking down past Marks & Spencer towards Ling's Tower, *c.* 1966.

Quinton Pool

This pool in Cheylesmore takes its name from the keeper of the Great Park (in which it lay), Thomas de Quinton. The spring-fed pool, originally a drinking place for deer, was once much larger and contained a large head of fish – at the beginning of the twentieth century it was stocked with trout. The pool also has a legend attached to it stating that it was once the home of a dragon that would come to the city wall and demand a sacrifice of a maiden. It is said to have come to Little Park Gate and clawed the stonework. These 'claw marks' – actually arrow-sharpening marks – were later shown as proof of the legend.

The dragon's 'claw marks' on the city wall. In reality these were probably arrow-sharpening marks from compulsory archery practice.

Richard III

During Henry VI's illness in 1453 Richard III's father, Richard, Duke of York, was made Protector of England. He later plotted against the king and in 1455 Henry moved to Coventry for his own safety. While here he removed York from his post. York tried his hand at the Battle of St Albans, where Henry was injured and shortly after relapsed into illness so York resumed as Protector. When Henry recovered in 1456 he moved the royal court to the safety of walled Coventry. Coventry became the base of government and the court for around three years – the king's capital.

In 1459 York was declared a traitor at the great council in Coventry Priory. Later in November, Henry's queen, Margaret of Anjou, summoned Parliament to Coventry Priory to punish the Yorkist. Cecily, York's wife, and his sons Richard (later king) and George (later Duke of Clarence) came as prisoners. This was probably Richard's first visit to Coventry.

York and other Yorkists were attainted, removing their rights, lands and property, the first act of this type in Parliament. A year later York's head was presented to Queen Margaret on a platter wearing a paper crown. The war ended with York's son being crowned Edward IV. Henry VI was murdered in the Tower and Queen Margaret ransomed back to the King of France. The last time the couple saw each other was in Coventry.

Later Richard of Gloucester became king. He and his brother George were attributed with killing Henry VI's son; Richard alone was attributed with Henry's murder. In St Mary's Guildhall hangs the Coventry Tapestry, sitting below the King's Window, creating one of the last major vestiges of the veneration of King Henry left in England.

The tapestry contains images of Henry VI, Queen Margaret and their son, Prince Edward. It also bears an image of Richard III, placed here as a piece of propaganda. He is placed looking out from the tapestry, showing his uneven shoulders, which were once thought of as propaganda but are now known to be fact. The line of saints have a gap over Richard's head – just a small snake-like squiggle appears.

In one hand he holds a pile of coins, the symbol of the Judas. This device, used since at least the fifteenth century, was attributed to Richard for Sir William Cecil

Above left: Margaret of Anjou from the Coventry Tapestry. She was presented with Richard's father's head.

Above right: When the tapestry was made Henry VI was called the 'Light of the World'.

Right: Richard III, shown here with his left shoulder slightly higher than the right and with his trademark crooked hand.

(Elizabeth I's secretary) said, 'Richard the third, he was Judas the Second.' In the closing moments of Shakespeare's *Richard III*, Richard compares himself to Judas.

In his left hand he appears to have once held a snake, which slips down and kisses the other hand holding the coins. The snake – a symbol of evil, cunning and manipulation – gives the kiss of the serpent to the hand, the sign of being in league and amity with Richard. The emblem, considered unlucky, was removed but its shadow remains.

In Shakespeare's *Richard III*, Queen Margaret says of Richard, 'this dog, whose bite is like an evil snake'. Sir Thomas More said Richard had destroyed his own mother, 'viper-like'. Sir Thomas wrote his history of Richard between 1514 and 1515, and during his research visited his sister in Coventry. He would have found his way into the Guildhall where the archives were stored and probably shown Richard on the tapestry. He later produced a painting of Richard known as the 'Broken Sword Portrait' that bears an uncanny resemblance – as if copied from the Coventry Tapestry.

Although made in the reign of Henry VII, it actually commemorates Coventry's greatest moment when it became the home to the royal court and the home of a saint – Henry was considered a saint by the people, with twenty-three Vatican-proven miracles. In the tapestry he looks up at the vision he saw for three years running: the Assumption of the Virgin and Christ in Glory (latter covered in the 1500s).

Richard suffered from Tudor propaganda, as he does in the tapestry, where he stands between two of his supposed victims. Ultimately he was placed there to show that Henry VII killed the man who killed the Lancastrian line, the prince and the saint. This followed Henry VII's vilification of Richard from 1485. Richard's image in the tapestry is thought to be possibly the oldest in existence and even shows a hair colour more in line with recent DNA tests.

S

St John the Baptist

Standing on oak piles driven into the old lake bed, the 'Babbu Lacu', St John's today sits around 14 inches above water in Fleet Street – derived from the old English *fleot*, meaning 'to float'. Queen Isabella gave ground to the Guild of St John to build a chapel in 1355 in which priests could pray for her soul and that of her murdered husband, Edward II. In 1357 it was served by two priests, one of which – Robert de Whoream – lived in a hermitage attached to it. By 1461 there were twelve priests. The church was used and maintained by the United Guild of the Holy Trinity based in St Mary's Hall. In the days of the guilds there were five altars: the High Altar and others dedicated to St John the Baptist, the Virgin Mary, St Catherine and the Holy Trinity. These were the guilds that formed the Trinity Guild. The priests lived within the college precincts and the college took up the area of the present quadrangle. Attached to this college was also the guilds' school.

In December 1547 an act suppressed all colleges, chapels, chantries and guilds. Holy Trinity Guild was suppressed and the church and contents given to the Corporation for

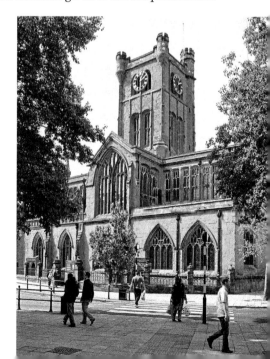

The Church of St John the Baptist in Fleet Street. This church still contains a bone of St Valentine in its altar.

a penny a year. The church was put to various uses and from 1607 occasional services continued. It was used as a prison for Scottish prisoners during the Second Civil War, and also as a market and stretch house among other things. In 1734 it reopened as the parochial church of the newly formed Parish of St John. It was restored in 1841 and again in 1868–76. During this period the original exterior of grey sandstone was clad with local red sandstone.

St Mary's Hall

Building began on the finest guildhall in Britain in 1340. The first half-timbered stage was built by the merchant guild of St Mary as a meeting place and banqueting hall; its kitchens are the oldest in England. This guild amalgamated with the guilds of St John, St Catherine and Holy Trinity, becoming the united guild of the Holy Trinity. Enriched, it began the second phase, which started in 1394 and ended in 1414 leaving the hall basically as it is today. The Trinity Guild became one of the most powerful guilds in England and traded across Europe. Noted members included Henry V, Henry VI and Henry VII.

Coventry was granted its Charter of Incorporation in 1345 and the most powerful in the city formed the first council and chose the first mayor. Practically all were guild members and the hall took on its secondary role as a council house, which ended in the late nineteenth century. The Trinity Guild association ended in 1547 when it was dissolved.

The hall has a remarkable history. Rebuilt from the remains of Coventry Castle, an entrance tower (mostly rebuilt) stands at the rear. It has been a meeting place for

The wonderful entrance to St Mary's Hall is decorated with the Virgin, a green man and angels.

kings, queens, the rich and the poor. It was also a theatre, the mystery plays were rehearsed here, and Shakespeare played here on numerous occasions as did the great Georgian actress Sarah Siddons.

The great hall was used as a courtroom, which George Eliot, a frequent visitor, used it for the trial of Hetty Sorrell in *Adam Bede*. She describes the north window, tapestry, gallery and armour. Other famous visitors too numerous to mention include Jane Austen and Charles Dickens. Nobility often visited, including Henry V who feasted here with his queen after Agincourt. His son Henry VI was a regular visitor, his badge covers the ceiling of the great hall. Henry VII also feasted here. Mary Queen of Scots was held in the Old Mayoress's Parlour and her son, James I, ate here as did his daughter, the Princess Elizabeth, and later James II.

The hall has many treasures including medieval roof bosses, the Great Chair, armour and the north window (dating around 1492) venerating Henry VI and his ancestors. Its greatest treasure is hanging beneath: the Coventry Tapestry, a unique piece made between 1495 and 1500. The tapestry and stained glass above are probably the last major surviving relic of the cult of Henry VI in England. It depicts 'Saint' Henry of Windsor, the second most venerated image in Tudor England after the Virgin. Over 300 miracles were attributed to the dead king, but his sainthood failed because of Henry VII's tight purse. One recent visitor wrote, 'I can honestly say ... our capital has nothing to compare to this beautiful medieval building.'

The Great Hall, looking from the armour-lined Minstrels' Gallery. Beyond lays the north window and the Coventry Tapestry – a national treasure.

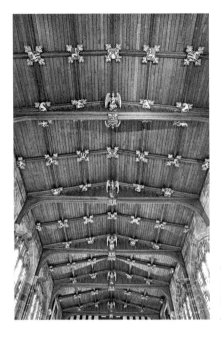

The ceiling of the Great Hall is covered in fourteenth- and fifteenth-century oak carvings, including the arms of Henry VI and Margaret of Anjou.

St Michael & All Saints

The first church here was a chapel dedicated to St Michael, built by Ranulf, Earl of Chester, which was given to the monks of Coventry Priory in 1135. The Langley Cartulary, in the early 1200s, refers to it as 'Saint Michael in the Bailey'. This relates to the fact that it lay within the bailey ditch of the earl's castle. Foundations have been found opposite St Mary's Hall and the south porch is said to be the oldest surviving section. Just east of the south porch lie massive foundations, likely castle remains edging along the northern castle ditch, which runs through the centre of the ruins.

By the beginning of the thirteenth century the Norman chapel had been replaced by a larger Early English church in the Decorated style. Little survives of the smaller building except a Decorated door arch in the south porch. The fourteenth century was the main building period. In 1373, work started on the steeple and the spire was added in 1432 as work continued in other parts. Coventry merchants William and Adam Botoner are said to have expended £100 annually building it. The spire was paid for by their sisters Ann and Mary.

The tower and spire, declared a masterpiece by Sir Christopher Wren, is the third tallest in England. It is unique because, unlike its two rivals Salisbury and Norwich, it is the highest tower/spire in the land built from the ground, not springing from the centre of the church. The tower, octagon and spire is adorned with forty-two kings, saints, confessors and benefactors. It measured 295 feet 9.5 inches, although after the 1880 restoration it was shortened to 294 feet – 3 inches longer than the church. The choir and body of the church, paid for by Ann and Mary Botoner, were built around

St Michael's, the old cathedral, as it was in around 1920.

A painting by Fred Roe showing George V visiting the ruined building in November 1940.

The ruins as they appear today.

the same time as the tower. In 1450 Henry VI heard Mass here. James I visited in 1617, and James II visited in 1687 touching 200 people for the king's evil.

The Collegiate Church of St Michael was made a cathedral in 1918. On the night of 14 November 1940 the cathedral was gutted by incendiaries. The following day its stone mason, Jock Forbes, clambered over the rubble, picked up two burned roof timbers, wired them together and formed a cross and placed it in the rubble where the altar had stood. Later it was placed on a new altar with the words 'Father Forgive' carved behind.

A recent £1 million restoration scheme to stabilise the ruins was funded by the World Monuments Fund and others after the building was listed as threatened in 2012. On its completion the dean said, 'It is a privilege to care for the iconic ruins.' This good work has been threatened recently by constant use of the ruins as a venue, including loud house music events. The cathedral's website states, 'Today the ruins of the old Cathedral are preserved as a memorial and sacred space for the City.'

St Michael (New Cathedral)

On 4 November 1944 the *Coventry Standard* reported, 'The reasons put forward for not restoring the old cathedral seem totally Inadequate to most Coventry citizens ... Coventry citizens object to the proposed new cathedral on many grounds, and primarily they deprecate the undemocratic attempt which is being made to rush the matter through ... What we want is restoration.'

Industrialist Sir Alfred Herbert offered to pay towards its restoration but those who led the city had little interest in the past, only wishing to look to the future – whether people liked it or not. Giles Gilbert Scot's design was released in 1944. Under

The new St Michael's, showing Epstein's St Michael and the Devil by the steps. Epstein modelled the head of the Devil on himself.

Looking from the altar towards the west screen, which is actually on the south.

pressure from the new bishop to design a modern building and from the Royal Fine Arts Commission to create a medieval one, he was forced to blend them. Unhappy, he resigned in 1947. His remarkable design incorporating the old cathedral is now forgotten

A competition was held to find a new design. There were 219 entrants and a relatively unknown Basil Spence won. Spence said while visiting the ruins he had seen a vision through a north window of the new building. It proved to be one of his most controversial works and is loved by some, hated by others. Time, however, makes modernity less harsh and in 1999 it was voted Britain's best-loved building.

The tapestry forms a backdrop to the altar. The main figure is Christ with a life-sized man at his feet. Until recently, it was the largest tapestry in the world.

Building work began 1954 and in May 1962 it was consecrated. Attached to the old building by a porch, it has massive sheer walls inspired by Norman cathedrals and the internal vaulting is like medieval Gothic. Jacob Epstein's bronze of St Michael and the Devil dominates the entrance and beyond is John Hutton's beautiful glass west screen decorated with saints, angels and Apostles. Hutton's ashes are buried at the base of his work. As you enter the building, beyond the slender columns and impressive vaulted ceiling is Graham Sutherland's massive tapestry of Christ in Majesty. To its right, John Piper's beautiful Baptistery Window has 195 panels of stained glass. Designed by Piper and made by Patrick Reyntiens, this stunning work depicts the light of God sweeping through the darkness into the world. Whatever people think of this building, it is not difficult to find beauty here.

Siege

There is a lot of confusion regarding the siege of Coventry. A recent book stated that Charles I summoned Coventry on 13 August 1642. In the National Army Museum there is a warrant signed and sealed by the king on 13 August at Nottingham. In the warrant he asked Lord Willoughby to raise a force to act as the king's lifeguard, consisting of 1,500 foot and 500 dragoons. When Charles was accused of levying war against his people, this letter proved incriminating as it was with this force he headed south. The Iter Carolinum, a diary of one of the royal attendants, informs us that the king was still in Nottingham on 16 August. On the 18th he went to Leicester, staying until the 19th then moved into Warwickshire, arriving at Stoneleigh Abbey on the same day.

Charles I lost Coventry and eventually his head.

Meanwhile, Coventry was choosing sides. The city recorder, Spencer Compton, Earl of Northampton, informed the king that he would hold the city for him. He secured the powder magazine in Spon Gate, but it was retaken and moved to Warwick Castle. Northampton had followers in the city and tried to raise more. Desperation ensued as 400 armed men from Birmingham arrived into the city. Coventry could now go only one way: for Parliament. As Northampton tried to raise support in the Bull Inn in Smithford Street, he was forced to flee. He headed straight for the king at Stoneleigh to inform him of the state of play.

The following day – the 20th – Charles summoned the city, demanding its subjugation:

Whereas diverse persons ill affected to his Majesties person and government, and strangers to this City of Coventry, are lately gotten into that city with arms and ammunition, who, with others of that place ill affected to the peace of this Kingdom, have combined to keep the said City by force of arms against his Majesty, their Liege Lord and Sovereign. For reducing of whom to their due obedience his Majesty hath given orders to some Commanders of his Forces to assault the said City, and by force to enter the same. Notwithstanding his Majesty being very unwilling, for some disaffected persons, to punish his good subjects and ruin his said City, is graciously pleased thereby to declare, that in case the said Strangers shall forthwith, after the publishing of the His Proclamation, depart peaceably out of the said City and they and the inhabitants presently lay down their arms, that then his Majesty will pardon as well all the said Strangers, as well as all other the Inhabitants of the said City. But if they shall persist in their said Action of Rebellion then his Majesty is resolved to proceed against them as Traitors and Rebels, and to use all extremity for reducing the said City to due obedience.

Given at our Court at Stonely Abbey the twentieth day of August, in the eighteenth year of our Reign, 1642.

As the king's army (estimated around 1,500) broke camp his herald, Sir William Dugdale, brought the king's demand to the city. After a short consultation he was informed that 'his Majesty's royal person should be most respectfully welcomed, but we could not with safety permit his cavaliers to enter the town'. Knowing the king would not enter alone, this was amended so the king could enter but with only 200 followers. Not a man to be dictated to, Charles sent to Northampton for siege weapons and set his cannons upon Park Hill on the brow of Little Park Quarry. The king's tent is said to have been erected in the Great Park so he could rest in comfort while his guns played on New Gate.

A Parliamentary pamphlet relating to events between 22 and 26 August 1642 says,

> The Houses [of Parliament] also received letters informing them of the true state of things at Coventry. That his Majesty continued his siege and battered against the town from Saturday till Monday last. That the cavaliers, with their pieces of ordnance, having battered down one of the gates, the townsmen, to prevent their entrance, stopped up the passage with harrows, carts and pieces of timber, and with great courage forced the cavaliers (notwithstanding their ordnance) upon every attempt towards the gate soon to retreat, and that with the same loss.

This appears to be an accurate report as it is backed up by John Vicars in the *Parliamentary Chronicle*, written shortly after the event, which has the following:

> The king ... drew up his forces before the city, planted his ordnance against its gate, which, by continually playing thereon, at last they battered and brake open ... Notwithstanding the valiant townsmen stoutly maintained the breech in the very mouth of the enemy's cannon; and to prevent their entrance with their horse, they stopt up the passage with harrows, carts and pieces of timber, laid crosswise on heaps, and ... forced the cavaliers ... to retreat with loss every time ... and little or

This view gives an idea of how a seventeenth-century army would have looked gathering outside Coventry.

none to themselves, so thick and quick discharges they made upon them with their musquet shots ... before the gate was broken open, some shot of their cannon, not rightly levelled, beat down a part of the Lady Hales house, in White-Fryers in the City, the said lady and an old woman, who had lain bed-ridden five years before in a place called the Tower, were both of them slain ... when the King's forces were retired, the incessant shot of the city falling like hail upon them, these resolute citizens and soldiers, with one unanimous consent, sallied out of the city, and behaved in such a valiant and undaunted manner, that they compelled the King's forces to retire with more than ordinary pace, forsaking their ordnance, which they cleared of all incumbrances, took two of them from the enemy, fiercely encountering the Cavaliers, and gave them such a shock and violent charge, that in a short time three score and ten of them lay slain on the ground; the rest were forced to a shameful and hasty retreat ... The king also retreated from this unexpected attack of the citizens of Coventry, to his forces which were collected at Leicester.

Other reports state that seventy Royalists were killed. John Rous said the army shot into the town, killing one man, and the town issued out. The rest of Rous' account matches the previous two, which appear to give us the truth behind the siege of Coventry.

The attack on Coventry lasted from Saturday 20th, when the city was summoned, until Monday 22 August, after the king decided on a strategic withdrawal after suffering a counter-attack and knowing that 10 miles away Lord Brooke and Colonel Hampden was heading for Coventry with a superior force. Nehemiah Wharton, a subaltern

The view the army would have seen. The large tree on the mound on the right was later put there to mark where the king had set up his tent.

officer in Essex's army, was in the force and wrote to his master of the events. In a letter dated 26 August 1642, written at Coventry, Wharton says, 'Monday morning (August 22nd) we marched into Warwickshere with about three thousand foote and four hundred horse'. Relief was on its way and the siege had ended.

Sent to Coventry

St John's has a well-known story attached to it: that of the phrase 'sent to Coventry'. Most have heard the story that when Scottish prisoners held there they were exercised in the street and Coventrians refused to talk to them, hence the phrase. There are problems with this: the link with the Civil War comes simply from a reference relating to some prisoners being sent or moved to Coventry from Birmingham. Also, in those days the quadrangle was still there so any prisoners being exercised wouldn't have gone into the streets. The most amazing thing about this story is that if you actually try to trace its origins it didn't exist beyond the 1930s – it is a modern tale. The true origins of the phrase 'sent to Coventry' lie in the city's past as a garrison city when soldiers stayed in inns, got drunk, got girls pregnant, got into fights and even occasionally killed people. During this time, before the building of the barracks in 1792, the saying is actually recorded and locals, especially girls, would not fraternise with the soldiers, hence the real origins of the phrase.

A foot soldier in the 1740s. It was soldiers such as this who created the problems that originated the saying 'sent to Coventry'.

Coventry Barracks, built in 1792, brought the soldiers under better control and integrated them into the city. My great-gran married one of the men in the picture.

Siddons, Sarah

The famous theatrical family the Kembles were regular players for sometimes up to six months in Coventry, performing dramas, comedies and even musicals. It was while engaged with her father in a series of performances at the Drapers' Hall that Sarah Kemble, on the morning of 25 November 1773, married William Siddons, then eighteen years old, at Holy Trinity. Sarah's father had forbidden her from marrying an actor but Sarah simply said, 'Father you can hardly call him an actor!'

Trinity's register reads:

> 1773: William Siddons, of the Parish of St. Michael's, and Sarah Kemble, of this parish, were married in this church by licence this 25th day of November, in the year One Thousand Seven Hundred and Seventy Three by me George Richards.—Signed, William Siddons, Sarah Kemble, in the presence of Roger Kemble, Mary T. Godfrey.

The ceremony was performed by Richards in the absence of Revd Joseph Rann, vicar of Holy Trinity. Rann was a Shakespearean scholar who reissued Shakespeare's work with notes. Little did he know at the time that he could have married England's future greatest Shakespearean actress.

Sarah Siddons, greatest actress of her time.

In 1805, Sarah played St Mary's Hall and in 1811 she played her last farewell to Coventry at the Theatre Royal in Smithford Street. Her part on that occasion was Lady Macbeth, and hundreds gathered to witness her entry into the theatre.

Skidmore, Francis

Francis Alfred Skidmore, born in Coventry in 1816, became one of the world's greatest art metalworkers. An apprentice to his father, he studied ancient metalwork and architecture and by 1850 he had set up his own business in West Orchard. From this time he began to be recognised for the beauty of his work. One of his earliest was the Hereford Screen for Hereford Cathedral, which after years of being stored away in Coventry is now a prize exhibit at the V&A.

Skidmore created the lighting for Holy Trinity and was also a warden and vestryman there. His work can be seen in twenty-four cathedrals including Canterbury, Westminster, York and St Paul's. It is also found in over 300 parish churches, castles and public buildings, and as far away as America and South Africa. His most conspicuous work was for Sir Gilbert Scott on the Albert Memorial in Hyde Park. Scott said of him, 'For the execution of the metalwork, comprising more than half of the monuments, the only man in the world to my knowledge to carry out my ideas was Mr Skidmore of Coventry, and he has done so.'

In later years he moved to Raglan Street, then Alma Street and later Meriden. Around 1893 he returned to Coventry and took up residence in Eagle Street. He later became partly blind and during this period was called to London to add to the railings on the Thames Embankment – his work. During this visit, due to his poor vision he was run over by a carriage. Afterwards, his business and his finances began to fail and he continued with support of the city freemen. He died on 13 November 1896, living in humble circumstances in Eagle Street and was buried in London Road Cemetery.

Above left: Francis Skidmore, one of Britain's greatest art metal artists.

Above right: Skidmore's metal pulpit in St Michael's Church was destroyed in the Blitz.

Spon Street

The scheme that began in 1967 proposed relocating buildings from various streets in the city. Eventually only properties in Much Park Street and western and central Spon Street were allocated to the Spon Street Townscape Scheme. The first restored in 1969 was No. 169, followed by the first relocated building, No. 9, previously No. 7 Much Park Street, which was re-erected in June 1972. The completed street was finished in 1990 and contained twelve buildings restored in situ and ten re-erected from other sites. Spon Street now has one of the most important groupings of medieval timber-framed buildings in the country.

Nos 1 and 2, dating from the fifteenth century (the last built), stand at the entrance to the street. Both formerly stood beyond the ring road. They were originally four hall houses known as Wealden houses. Wealden houses are normally bigger but the Coventry version was adapted for smaller spaces. There are more Wealden houses here than any street in England.

Nos 11–12, with its oriel windows, was built in the mid-fourteenth century and is probably the oldest remaining building standing on its original site. It's an incomplete Wealden house with a central hall. Nos 14 and 15, known as the Tudor House, dates to the fifteenth century and was formerly the Recruiting Sergeant inn. Nos 20 and 21, formerly Nos 122–123 Much Park Street, has a fifteenth-century front and sixteenth-century back, was originally the Green Dragon Inn, made famous by George Eliot's novel *Middlemarch*.

Nos 1 and 2 Spon Street, the last built.

A fourteenth-century Wealden house in Spon Street, with its double oriel windows.

The Old Windmill, known as Ma Brown's from former publican Ann Brown, is a plastered timbered building dating from at least the sixteenth century. It was originally two buildings; the entrance originally led into a narrow courtyard that divided them. The left side was a shop into the late nineteenth century. The original Windmill was on the right and is not to be confused with the older Windmill Inn in Spon Causeway. Among these buildings stand others original to the street.

Swanswell

Swanswell Pool originated as part of the ancient Babu Lacu lake, which filled the central lower section of Coventry. Legend has it that the 'Swineswell' was created by the rutting of a giant boar that was killed by Sir Guy of Warwick. The blade bone of this boar, sometimes claimed as the blade bone of the Dun Cow, hung for many years on Gosford Gate. In the early nineteenth century the bone was said to have been cast into the pool.

Up until the late nineteenth century the pool froze over winter and it was one of the best-known places for ice skating in the city. There was a hermit's hut on the island where the proprietor of the Swanswell Tavern served refreshments and provided a fire and seats for the skaters to rest upon. At the west end of Swanswell Pool the footpath divided. The main path ran to Swanswell Gate and an offshoot followed the course of Bird Street. In the angle formed was Little Swanswell Pool, a smaller pool that disappeared when the neighbourhood was developed.

33130. COVENTRY, SWANSWELL & HOSPITAL

Swanswell Pool in 1905 showing the island used to serve refreshments to skaters.

Terry, Ellen

Ellen Terry, the greatest actress of her time, was born here on 27 February 1847 while her parents were on tour. The location of her birthplace has been a matter of conjecture for years. When she visited in 1906 she said her mother told her, 'you go into Market Street and the house is on the right-hand side.' When asked which end of Market Street should be entered to get the correct right-hand side she laughed and said, 'That's where madness lies.' The editor of the *Coventry Standard* told her he thought it was No. 5.

Pilgrims visiting pleaded for the right information, but only confusion was forthcoming. One shop bore a plaque stating, 'This is the birthplace of Ellen Terry'. Directly opposite stood another shop with another plaque, which claimed: 'This is the original birthplace of Ellen Terry'. One – No. 26 – was a haberdashers while the other – No. 5 – was a tripe shop. The vicar of Holy Trinity told her it was not the tripe

Dame Ellen Terry dressed to play Lady Macbeth.

shop, but he was probably just being nice. When Terry's daughter visited, she placed a daffodil in both shops.

The mystery had actually been resolved back in January 1893. No. 26, called The Ellen Terry House, was pushed as the birthplace and thousands of theatre lovers visited it. In that year the fruiterer (then opposite at No. 5) put his plaque outside, stating that his shop was Ellen Terry's birthplace. Three weeks later a sign in No. 26 claimed, 'This house is the original birthplace of Miss Ellen Terry and no other.' The press visited and the owner, Mr Needle, said that the shop opposite was a local tradesman at the time of her birth and their shop was a lodging house.

The following day the reporter made contact with the nurse who brought Dame Ellen into the world. She still had a 'lively recollection' and said the birth actually took place at No. 5 Market Street, which at the time was occupied by Mr and Mrs Wilson. She stated that Mrs Wilson was well known to theatricals who visited and she let rooms to them. Opposite, she recalled, were other lodgings kept by Mrs Faulkener, who only let her rooms to gentlemen lodgers and did not provide apartments for actors.

The nurse added, 'there is no doubt about the matter, Mr and Mrs Terry took apartments at the house of Mrs Wilson, 5 Market Street.' A few days later Mrs Wilson came knocking on her door, saying Mrs Terry had taken ill unexpectedly. The nurse went to her assistance and the day ended with the birth of one of the greatest actresses to grace the stage. The nurse continued to visit and said Mr Terry had to move on with the troupe, leaving his wife and baby behind. A few weeks later Mrs Terry followed in a carriage procured by the nurse's husband, who worked in the nearby Castle Hotel. The nurse assisted them into the carriage and waved them off. It was the last time she saw the child, but always followed Ellen's career.

According to the 1851 census the Wilsons were simply listed as a newsagent, presumably at that time with no one in their rooms. Mrs Faulkener is described as a laundress with two male lodgers, exactly in the manner the nurse remembered!

This image, taken in 1938, shows Mayor Alice Arnold in the doorway of Tripey Hayes shop. The lady by her, Phyllis Neilson-Terry, stands with 'Tripey'. It was pointed out that the shop opposite also had a plaque claiming it as the birthplace.

Despite the testimony of Dame Ellen's nurse, No. 26 continued to call itself the 'Ellen Terry House', and even as late as 1901 promoted this fact in the newspapers. In 1938 when Terry's niece visited, actress Phyllis Neilson-Terry, both houses still bore their respective plaques and continued to until they were blitzed on 14 November 1940. A blue plaque was later placed on one of the ramps on the Upper Precinct.

Thornton, John

John Thornton of Coventry was an early fifteenth-century English international Gothic glass painter. He is thought to have been active between 1405 and 1433, mostly in his native Coventry and York. His workshop in Coventry was in St John's Bridges, the Burges. He was contracted to create the east window in York Minister in 1405, the largest stained-glass window in Europe. He also made works for buildings in Coventry and smaller commissions in northern England. There were 5,000 loose pieces of glass, some Thornton removed from the old cathedral in 1939. The new cathedral also houses complete Thornton panels in the undercroft. Other pieces survive in Coventry's Guildhall.

Art historians around the world recognise John Thornton as one of the greatest and most influential of all medieval artists, and the Great East Window in York is his largest surviving work; its importance and global reputation is unmatched.

A fragment of glass in the south aisle of St Michael's showing a fine Thornton angel.

True Blue

The making of non-fading dark blue thread and cloth was once a flourishing industry here, and it became famous on account of the permanence of the dye, bringing about the saying 'as true as Coventry blue'. In the ancient play *George a Green*, written nearly 500 years ago, two of the characters state:

Jenkin: And she gave me a shirt collar, wrought over with counterfeit stuff.
George: What! Was it gold?
Jenkin: Nay, it was better than gold!
George: What was it?
Jenkin: Right Coventrie Blue!

In the play *The Vow Breaker*, written in 1636, Miles the miller speaks of his handkerchief as being sewed with 'Coventre'. Many regulations were made for the prevention of fraud in the spinning and selling of this blue thread and cloth. Twenty years later and the making of blue thread and cloth was lost to the city and foreign imports took over.

Although not true blue (as no known samples survive), this is a silk that superseded cloth weaving. This is by Thomas Stevens, Coventry's most famous silk picture manufacturer.

Underground

Around 1900 the children of the landlord of the New Inn in Gosford Street were playing in an upper room when a panel slid down on a wall, exposing a shaft going underground. The panel was grooved and held up by an old latch. Someone was lowered down and found a table set up with two chairs at the bottom. The finders came to the conclusion that it was a hiding place from the Civil War, while another story put forward was that Dick Turpin hid here. Tradition says Turpin was in Coventry staying at the Rose and Crown (Courtyard) in High Street. It was actually reported in Turpin's day that he had been taken in Coventry, but this proved untrue.

Not the shaft – it's long gone or hidden – but this is the secret cellar of the Star Inn in Earl Street.

V

'V'

The 'V' was a common mark use by some stonemasons to mark their work for payment. Such marks can be seen around the tower of St Michael and in the undercroft of St Mary's Hall. The rarer use of the linked double-scratched V can be seen in the treasury in Caesar's Tower of St Mary's Hall. This is a ritual magic protection mark, meaning Virgin Virginatis and was actually believed to invoke the Virgin Mary to protect whatever it was scratched on. The tower was mostly blown up in 1940 but the small surviving section of wall in the room has nine visible surviving 'VV' marks on it. The question is did the magic fail, resulting in the destruction of the tower or was the surviving section the only area marked and thus protected?

One of a number of 'VV' ritual marks in Caesar's Tower.

Watchmaking

Samuel Watson, friend of Samuel Pepys, was Coventry's earliest recorded watch- and clockmaker. He was also a noted mathematician. He initially came to Coventry around 1680. He was sheriff in 1686, then as his fame grew he moved to London around 1691. Watson was made a Free Brother of the Clockmaker's Company in 1692. In 1682, while still in Coventry, Watson made a remarkable astronomical clock for Charles II followed by another clock, which was not completed until after the king's death. In 1690, this same clock was sold to Queen Mary and is now in Windsor Castle. Watson also made two astronomical clocks for his friend Sir Isaac Newton and invented five-minute repeating watches.

Throughout the eighteenth and nineteenth centuries Coventry became one of the main centres of watchmaking in the country and by 1860 there were ninety watch manufacturers in the city. In that same year the Free Trade Act allowed the importation of cheap American watches, which damaged the trade. It never quite recovered, leaving only manufacturers such as Rotherham.

Thomas Chapman,
watchmaker in
Priory Row.

A beautiful chain-driven watch, minus its gold case, by Thomas Loseby of Coventry.

Whitefriars

The Carmelites, or Whitefriars, came to Coventry in 1342 aided by Sir John Poultney, Mayor of London. Dedicated to the Virgin Mary, the friars wore white robes and their friary (the Convent of Our Lady of Mount Carmel, also known as Whitefriars) with its church stood in 10 acres. It was a centre of theology and music, and the friary held a large library. The friars lived an austere lifestyle, were popular and received many gifts. Despite this austerity their 303-foot-long central towered church was likened to a small cathedral, being one of the largest friary churches in England. They attended services every three hours – day and night. Some of their choir stalls survive today in the Old Grammar School. When not at services they preached, taught and studied. One of its famous friars is William of Coventry, a fourteenth-century theologian and historical writer who was buried in the chapter house.

The friary maintained the city wall around their house and adapted a tower facing the London Road into a shrine called 'Our Lady of the Tower'. Inside was a painted chamber and an image of the Virgin, all who passed saluted it or visited it and gave contributions. It was on the list of major pilgrimage sites in England.

The house and its fourteen friars surrendered to the Crown in 1538. The church was sold to a member of the royal household, George Pollard and speculator Andrew Flamock, who sold it on in 1543 to Coventry Corporation who then knocked it down. The rest was granted to Sir Ralph Sadler who sold it in 1544 to John Hales (clerk of the hanaper and baronet) for £83 12s 6d.

Hales demolished some and turned the rest, including the cloisters, into his private residence known as Hales Place. Here he entertained Elizabeth I over three nights. The queen is said to have made a short speech from the oriel window. Mary Queen of Scots was kept here in 1569–70 and later her son James I stayed.

Whitefriars from the London Road side, showing its oriel window.

The building from the rear showing a blocked-up section.

It remained in the Hales family until the early eighteenth century, when it was purchased by the Duke of Montague who in 1722 sold it to Samuel Hill of Shenstone Park. It then passed to Mr Smith, a clergyman of Apsley, who sold it in 1801 to the Directors the Poor of the United Parishes of Coventry and it was converted into a workhouse. A good deal had been removed before 1800, but parts remained including the cloisters, which was used as the dining room for the inmates. Whitefriars was restored and became a museum in the 1960s, then became a museum storeroom. It is now under the Historic Coventry Trust.

Whitefriars Gate

Whitefriars Gate in Much Park Street is the postern gatehouse of Whitefriars Friary. It now consists of one dwelling with a central pointed arch leading into Whitefriars Lane. It was built in 1352 as the main entrance to the friary; Elizabeth I, Mary Queen of Scots and James I have all passed through its arch. The gate became the property of John Hales. The lane through the gate once ran to the inner gate of the friary, Bachelor's Gate, which was bombed in 1940.

Whitefriar's Gate from the rear.

It is associated with Charles Dickens for a scene in *The Old Curiosity Shop* is set here when Little Nell and her grandfather pulled their caravan into waste ground by the gate. The moon was shining, leaving the archway very black. Dickens noted an empty niche from which a statue had fallen. Quilp appeared through the arch and asked at what hour the London coach passed. Dickens knew the London coach passed here.

It was home to a popular toy museum, which closed over ten years ago. After a number of years of deterioration, restoration and deterioration the gate has now been passed to the Historic Coventry Trust.

Whittle, Sir Frank

Sir Frank Whittle has a permanent place in history. He is the original inventor of the turbo-jet engine, as described in his first patent, published in January 1930 (predating later previous claims) when he was only twenty-two years old. His invention revolutionised civil and military air transport the world over. Frank was born on 1 June 1907 at No. 72 Newcombe Road, Earlsdon. The son of Moses and Sarah Whittle, he was educated at Earlsdon Primary School and later Milverton council schools. He

The Whittle Arch.

learned much from his father, who worked in a Lancashire cotton mill from the age of eleven and had himself become a skilled mechanic and inventor.

As a child Frank flew his kite on nearby Hearsall Common. It was here in 1916 he saw an aeroplane land and on take-off it blew his hat into a gorse bush; this sparked his fascination with flight. His first attempts to join the RAF failed due to his lack of height, but he was accepted in 1923 as an apprentice. He qualified as a pilot officer in 1928.

While a cadet Whittle wrote a thesis arguing that if planes needed to achieve longer ranges they needed to fly at higher altitudes to avoid air resistance. Piston engines and propellers not being suitable, he suggested rocket propulsion or gas turbines driving propellers would be required. By October 1929, Whittle's mind had turned to jet propulsion and he considered using a fan enclosed in the fuselage to generate a fast flow of air to propel a plane at high altitude. A piston engine ate fuel, so he thought of using a gas turbine. The Air Ministry turned down his brilliant idea so he patented it himself.

In 1935, he secured financial backing and with Royal Air Force approval the company Power Jets Ltd was formed. They began constructing a test engine in July 1936. Whittle decided a complete rebuild was needed but lacked the funds to do it. Long negotiations with the Air Ministry followed and the project was eventually secured in 1940. By April 1941 the engine was ready for tests and had its first flight in a Gloster E.28/39 on 15 May 1941.

By October America was showing interest and asked for details and an engine. A Power Jets team with an engine was flown to Washington. The Americans worked quickly and their XP-59A Airacomet was flying in October 1942, some time before the British Gloster Meteor jet finally became operational in 1944. Whittle retired from the RAF in 1948 holding the rank of air commodore. He was knighted in the same year. He died in Canada on 9 August 1996.

The statue of Frank Whittle in Millennium Place.

X File

In March 1772 the papers recall that Mary Clews of Gosford Street was burnt to death by spontaneous combustion. She was 'excessively addicted to dram-drinking that she drank a quart of rum daily, thus filling her veins with spirits she became as inflammable as a lamp'. Mary Clews was a widow aged fifty-two and her health had gradually declined due to drinking. In February 1772 she took to her bed suffering from jaundice, according the surgeon to Mr Wilmer. She continued drinking.

Stoke St Michael as it was when Mary Clews was buried there.

On the morning of 2 March smoke was seen coming from her window and when her door was broken open flames were seen and quickly extinguished. Then a strange discovery was made: she lay between the bed and the fireplace, and with the exception of the legs and one thigh, there were no remains of any skin or muscles. The bones of the skull, thorax, spine, and the upper extremities were completely calcified and covered with a whitish efflorescence. Nearby furniture was untouched, as were the bedclothes and curtains.

Mr Wilmer said the only way he could account for this accident was that she had tumbled out of bed in the early hours of the morning and was set on fire either by the candle on the chair or a piece of coal falling from the grate, and the drink rendered her inflammable. The explanation was hardly likely and when she was buried flies although out of season swarmed her coffin until its burial in Stoke Churchyard.

York, Chester, Wakefield

Coventry, Chester and Wakefield have something in common: they are all famous for the production of mystery plays. The plays in Coventry may have started in the late thirteenth century and were linked to Corpus Christi processions. The production, which started at daybreak and ended at nightfall, was performed by the city's trade guilds on huge pageant waggons pulled to their stations by horses. After an early morning torchlight procession they began with the Creation, then the Deluge, then the birth of Christ. During one section, Joseph returns the child Christ to Mary and the Coventry Carol was sung. The life of Christ followed, ending with Doomsday (performed by the drapers) where a giant representation of the world was set alight

Pageant waggon outside Greyfriars Gate.

A mystery play being enacted beside the old Coventry Cross, built in 1541.

and the dead were judged with some cast into Hell's mouth by the Devil amid the cheers of the crowd. In the 1580s Coventry was becoming more puritanical and the plays were turned into a politically correct work called the *Destruction of Jerusalem*. This was first performed in 1584 and by 1589 the 400-year-old Coventry plays had been killed off. Modern versions have been performed by the Belgrade Theatre over a number of years.

Zoo

Coventry Zoo Park at Whitley was opened 4 April 1966, with admission at 3s for adults and 1s 6d for children. The zoo's opening ceremony was reported as follows:

> Pickles was king of beasts for the day ... A mongrel dog took the spotlight from lions, tigers, bears, and what is claimed to be the heaviest elephant in the country when Coventry Zoo Park was officially opened by the Lord Mayor, Ald. W. Parfitt, yesterday. Pickles, the mongrel that found the football World Cup, trotted up to Ald. Parffit with the key round his neck.

The well-remembered 60-foot 2.5-ton fibreglass statue of a Zulu warrior stood astride the zoo's entrance from March 1970. The zoo was set up by the Bank's, both previously show jumpers, with the help of the Chipperfield family. The couple from Surrey stayed in a caravan as the zoo was built up around them. Their elephant, Zukie, was forty years old and has previously worked as a log shifter in India. In 1966, Zukie led Coventry's carnival procession.

Zac, a six-year-old leopard, escaped his enclosure in 1972. Keepers attended with brooms while waiting for a tranquiliser gun from Dudley Zoo.